I0569207

"Descending to later ascend together"

UNION of SOULS

Barbro Curman

www.lightspira.com

Other titles by Barbro Curman:

Love Beyond Death, 2018
Head in Heaven, 2011

Titles by Mikael Curman:

Time Please, 2012

Published by LightSpira 2019
www.lightspira.com
ISBN: 978-91-86613-39-6

Author: Barbro Curman
Cover: Ulla Lindgren & Marie Örnesved
Coverphoto: Nataly Tverdovskaya
Pen illustration: Niklas Curman
Book Design: Marie Örnesved

© Copyright 2019, Barbro Curman
www.curmans.se
barbro@curmans.se

Contents

PROLOGUE

Welcome to *Union of Souls*. This is the second book in the trilogy about my husband Mikael's and my soul journey. It embraces the first five years after his death and it describes our meetings in the world of souls. Not only ours, but also meetings with other souls that have gone before us, who show us the way through their loving energy. This is how we mature and develop.

All of us have a Divine part within our soul. It is through this Divine part that all of humanity is one and the same consciousness. All souls will eventually be united in Divine consciousness. We come as individual souls many times to Earth to gather experiences and to mature. We often incarnate in groups that support each other in different ways. A great number of souls are contributing in their unique way to the Whole during this special time of Earth's transition. We all originate from the one heart of pure love. When a soul has learned what love is, and what love is not, then it can choose to return home along with its harvest of discoveries. Every soul's journey is beautiful in its own way and is uniquely contributing to the Whole.

The energy of the soul adheres to different physical laws than the ones we abide to on Earth, even if everything is energy also in the physical world. Every tree, stone, house and physical body is in essence energy. *Union of Souls* is about soul energies meeting earthly energies.

On Earth humans exist in a defined range of energy frequencies where time and space are reference points. Altered states, beyond physical frequencies, can be reached through meditation for example. Time and space then cease to exist. The development of the soul is about freeing oneself from the limitation of time and space, which is essentially a question of identification (with the body or with the soul). We can live on Earth and at the same time be more identified with our soul which of course has its implications, something you will learn about in this book.

At the end of 1990's Mikael and I connected with an infant researcher Dr Ed Tronick a pioneer in his field. He coined the concept The Dyadically Expanded Consciousness as something that arises in "Moments of Meetings". Dr. Tronick found regularities, patterns, in the non-verbal meeting between a six-month old child and its mother. During a "Moment of Meeting" two people share the same energy field. When they leave this meeting, both are enriched indefinitely. A meeting where both persons' consciousness expand in this way is only possible when they, in the moment, have let go of fears (see the literature list for further information).

Already when I got to know the concept, I intuitively knew that it was true also for the development of souls although Dr. Tronick's research was focused on the love between a mother and her child. A love that made both individuals' consciousness expand. Love transcends fear. Fear originates from the past and is projected onto the future. It is necessary to be present in the moment to create this shared energy field, which can happen when we open ourselves to the perspective of the soul.

When we are embraced by Mother Nature, when we meditate and let the light in, when we pray to Christ, Buddha or other Masters that have gone before us – then we share the same energy field and we are raised in energy. When that happens we can sense a certain kind of lightness and joy in our body.

There is right now a radical polarisation on Earth between those who choose to explore and live from a soul consciousness and the non-believers who separate themselves from the soul. I am one of those who have chosen to, through my own experiences and exploration, try to understand life's mysteries. More and more people are exploring spirituality beyond religions. Sceptics exist everywhere, particularly

10

within science and traditional religions. Bridge builders are very much needed.

Dr. Eben Alexander, a brain surgeon, who 2008 was hit by a life-threatening bacteria and ended up in a coma for seven days, is one of those extremely valuable bridge builders. He lost all brain functions and on day seven doctors considered removing all life-sustaining treatment.

Against all odds not only did he return to life, he also recovered completely and returned to his profession as a brain surgeon.

Dr. Alexander had during the coma intensive near-death experriences, which of course was mind-blowing in itself. However, more was to come. After recovering, he and his close colleagues, who had treated him, went through the medical records from his seven days in coma. When they realised that experiences like these, according to traditional brain science, would not be possible as his brain had been totally down-and-out, then Dr Alexander´s old view of the brain´s role in consciousness was totally torn to pieces.

Since then Dr Alexander has been engaged in researching the role and function of consciousness. Traditional brain research holds true that the brain is creating all experiences. Newer research suggests that consciousness exists beyond the brain.

Dr Alexander terms this theory *The Filter Theory* saying that the physical brain, in neocortex , serves as the reducing filter through which universal consciousness is filtered, or allowed in, to our more restricted perception of the world around us.

We can in meditative states and higher consciousness go beyond the brain´s limitations and thus become part of a greater collective consciousness (for more information, see the literature list).

In my book *Head in Heaven* I describe how my 'soul brother' after his death guided me to the Etheric School of Master Kuthumi. I was through inner tender meetings invited to share their energy field. I was awoken every night for many years to receive teachings. My consciousness expanded, preparing me for what was to come.

It was thanks to this training that I, in energy, could receive my great love and husband Mikael a few weeks after his death. To my great surprise he came as a wild and passionate soul energy. This was the introduction to our soul marriage where we share the same energy field between the dimensions. In my book *Love Beyond Death* I tell about the first one and a half years after Mikael's death. What happened was totally beyond my control. If I got stuck grieving, then the frequency lowered, and I lost our connection. The same happened if I was longing too much for our soul meetings. The only way was to stay open, be present and surrender fully to the higher forces.

Union of Souls is written from Mikael's perspective in our union between the dimensions. It is written through direct transmission in words from his soul to me, but above all through our ability to experience from each other's soul. The foundation was laid through the people we once were, our lives and work together during thirty years on Earth. Yet these people are just a fraction of an eternally vast energy field that gradually is opening up for us between the worlds. This is where our love now resides, enriched and refined with the loving guidance we have received.

The Prologue and the Epilogue encloses the story and is meant to facilitate your reading. You will find some words and terms that are underlined. Explanations to these words are offered in the chapter "Words and Concepts" at the back of the book. Throughout the book the perspectives of Barbro and Mikael are named B and M respectively. This emphasises that the meetings are between our soul energies, still linking to the persons we once were and in particular to me, Barbro who is still in a physical body.

Now I pass the word to M.

12

Thank you for your prologue, my dear!

It is a great wonder

being able to get my

voice out in

While

phys

INTRODUCTION

Thank you for your prologue, my dear! It is a great wonder being able to make my voice heard in this way. Such a thought would have been strange to me when I was still on Earth. So much is different now and I have gained a greater understanding of what our Universe is about. I sense a wisdom and love so enormous, yet impossible to embrace in full.

When I was living in physical form on Earth, I regarded myself as an atheist. A close friend of mine, a dean in my home town church, told me that he experienced me as an unusually spiritual atheist. Perhaps I was. What I reacted negatively towards was the ready-made answers from the different religions to the questions 'where do we come from?', 'why are we here?' and 'where are we going?'. I was on the other hand always interested in exploring these existential questions. Intuitively, I understood that our existence on Earth has a deeper meaning, than that which can be found in daily life.

Barbro can sense my energy and she perceives that which I wish to express in words. She does not see me in pictures as clairvoyants do. That would most likely have made the connection to our recent life together too strong, making her long for the physical closeness we once experienced. This would for sure obstruct our current communication. It is a great paradox. She has had to totally let go of me as a soul for me to choose my path. Barbro allowing me to be free is exactly why I can be close to her now. I have lived many lives in Tibet and I imagined my life beyond the physical returning to the eternal peace there. My path turned out to be a quite different one.

To my great wonderment I went directly into the Light after my physical death. I met there, among several other

16

light beings, Master Kuthumi, who had been guiding Barbro for many years. At this time I realized that I too, simultaneously, had been guided when on Earth, although in more subtle ways. Master Kuthumi now helped me see and understand the purpose of my life. It was put into perspective of many lives lived and in the light of the agreements Barbro and I as souls had made regarding these lives. I enjoyed embracing all this.

Leaving life on Earth is like being born into a new state of consciousness. The fact that Barbro and I were together during the time of transition, and that we were supported by our loving Masters, facilitated the crossing over. It felt like I was surfing on a wave with no resistance from the outside. I was free to move on.

To say farewell and allow loved ones to mourn the coming departure has its time. However, when the time is ripe for someone to be born into a new state of consciousness, then it is valuable to give space for that person to leave in a peaceful way.

Death is not what most people imagine. Our physical body is like a shell that is returned to Earth. Other shells, related to time and space, disappear as well. Our subtle energy bodies remain in a timeless state of consciousness. You can, when stilling yourself, learn to communicate through these subtle bodies into other dimensions of life. Every soul is unique, in the same way that every human on Earth is unique. Since my return into formlessness, my reverence for the whole of Creation has deepened enormously. I realize that we are like children in an eternal world of wisdom and love. I am deeply grateful for being part of all this in a conscious way. I know the same goes for Barbro.

On our soul journeys Barbro and I came to the midpoint of polarities; the experience that everything exists in everything, all is united in energy while at the same time the original quality, or essence, remains.

In this book I describe the path we took to reach that stage of consciousness. It is a path created and lived through ourselves enabled by our ever expanding ability to live from within each other's soul energy. We have come to the understanding that the Universe as a whole is created in the same way. Humanity is actually one and the same energy. It functions like a hologram, where the whole exists in every piece.

How is it possible to be in our different parts at the same time as we are a hologram? Because we are one and the same without beginning and end. There is no time where I am. Love is the force that holds the Universe together. Love is the same as Creation itself. Love creates abundantly and makes consciousness stretch itself to experience as much as possible. Our third dimension, built from polarities in time and space, is rich in possibilities. We can perceive the world as good or bad, powerful or weak. As we divide life into opposites we can learn from the experience of polarities.

In a dualistic world we often create with good intentions only to later realise that the opposite of what we created comes along in the process. We are now to a large extent destroying our own creations and learning in the third dimension has therefore come to its end. We have, through our lives on Earth, gathered wisdom and learnt what love is and what love is not. Time is ripe for the next wave of souls to return to the heart of the Universe together with their harvest of experiences. Other souls that have gone before, show us the way with their energy. Every soul has its unique journey to make in its own time. The rhythm is like a big breath in the Universe.

The key to the development of the soul is to dare receive unconditional love—love beyond polarities. Our hearts open when we let unconditional love in. Everything then proceeds naturally. Unconditional love inspires us, and it helps us face the fears that have kept us from expressing love. This is how personal love you experience on Earth is enriched with unconditional, _universal love_. The union of my soul with Barbro´s while she is physically on Earth, is our contribution to the Whole. Our years together as a physical couple created the foundation for what is now happening.

It is important that everything progresses in a natural way. If, for any reason, we get ahead of ourselves in our striving, the growth we are longing for is blocked. Even in so-called 'spiritual' environments there are tendencies to strive for states of consciousness and experiences beyond the earthly. All ambitions block the flow. It is good to remember that every soul is on its own unique journey and that we only can share experiences along the path. Our hope is to inspire you, a fellow soul traveller, to recognise your own soul's desire and path.

I am free!

Like a calf in spring approaching the green grass – that describes my first experience of coming over to what you on Earth call the 'other side'. One of our close friends described it in that way to B. In her inner mind, she had seen me running in a green meadow, free and happy. Leaving my physical body was a great relief to me, as it had been ill and heavy for many years. To my great wonder I was totally aware and conscious, although I was not yet used to living without a physical body.

I was welcomed and received help in navigating this new dimension. Master Kuthumi (who had been guiding B while we were both on Earth) was now my guide. Through him I understood the bigger picture and that he had been guiding me as well while I was in my physical body. He showed me how everything in the Universe is woven together into a whole, something that is impossible to comprehend with the type of intellect and way of thinking that are common on Earth.

Time and space do not exist where I am now. My physical body has been abandoned, but my subtle bodies remain. As souls our consciousness lives here in a timeless state and the consciousness of space is also totally different. As souls we are able to exist in many places simultaneously. We move by our thoughts. This is a great transformation compared to living on Earth in our physical body.

Master Kuthumi guided me and I was raised in energy. I had the opportunity to go through my latest life on Earth. Filled with wisdom and love, I was able to understand what I had learnt during that life. It also helped me to tender-hearted embrace situations that had been difficult. All this evoked a longing to communicate with my loved ones. Master Kuthumi told me the best way and I approached them, often in a dream. They felt my presence, and that to me was a great joy.

The bigger picture

To my great wonder I was shown how everything is connected. I understood that humanity and the Universe as we know it is like a single pulsating heart that we all come from. Overflowing love wishes to create. As human beings we have the opportunity to grow in soul and spirit. Dualism on Earth provides a way to learn through our own creations.

Between our different lives on Earth we exist where I am now. Here our souls mature and learn from our time on Earth. We are all souls making earthly experiences. We incarnate in groups of souls and we make different agreements within this group. It is not about details but about specific qualities we wish to develop further. These are holy contracts. However, we often don´t remember our agreements, when we are born on Earth. Everything is shown in glimpses, if and when, you open yourself to receiving them. Some human beings are open already as small children; others awaken later, often through crises.

Embracing this bigger picture, I understood the journey of my own soul through many lives on Earth and also why those lives had been different. My soul was to be prepared for what is happening now. Master Kuthumi taught that we as souls belong to what he termed 'cosmic families' and in this way we are ingeniously linked to one another. We learn from those who have walked before us on this path of love and we help those who need us in the same way. This makes us dependent on one another for the maturing of our souls and for humanity as a whole. Within a cosmic family, you often make agreements before you incarnate together. The aim is to assist one another to develop and in that way spread love and wisdom on Earth.

My agreements

The bigger picture brought a new light to my latest life on Earth. Especially evident and strong was my ability to understand the agreements I as soul had made before that life. During my last seven years on Earth I had a feeling of something special, but at that time I had no words to describe it. I was diagnosed with lung cancer and prepared myself to die. Seven years went by before it happened, which is rare and makes me grateful; they were an important seven years.

From this perspective, being here, I understood that my last seven years on Earth was about preparing the path to accomplish the agreements I had made before this life. It was clear to me that B and I have an old agreement that has sustained through many lives. Some of these lives we lived together, but in most of them not. Nonetheless, all these lives are parts of what is to be completed now. I also understood that we as souls both belong to the cosmic family of Master Kuthumi. That also goes for human beings who are close to us. One such person B calls her 'soul brother' who also was close to me while we both lived in physical bodies. Now when L and I both are here as souls, I realise that the links are even stronger. After his physical death, it was he who with great patience inspired B to open herself totally to the spiritual world. He was the one who guided her to the Etheric School of Kuthumi.

What was the best way to approach B and tell her what was now ahead of us? Our part of the divine plan, which all souls are part of, includes that we will unite as souls while she is still in her physical body on Earth. We have agreed, through our own process on our soul journey, to contribute to the union of Man & Woman and Heaven & Earth, all into one. It is about co-operation between dimensions.

24

We have great support in our commitment from souls all around us, both souls who live here and souls on Earth. Master Kuthumi showed me the way.

I was close to my dear ones when they were planning my funeral – there was so much love among them. Awakened and expressed love was the important thing, not my funeral as such. I was often present in our old home and with B. On one occasion, a few days after my passing, she was there working on her laptop. The external world is demanding also in the midst of grief. She discovered that a bird had come into the kitchen and refused to fly out through the open kitchen door. I, as soul energy, for a while went into the bird. She took it tenderly into her hands and let it fly out through the door. It didn't resist but felt safe in her hands. She must have felt my energy in the bird, because she said: 'Fly and be free!'

Freedom has always been precious to me, including freedom of the soul. B knew of, and shared, my values. The last thing she wished to do was to risk keeping me heavy and bound to Earth due to her grief. When she within herself asked me about this, I immediately answered:

– *You are not able to!*

My words were accompanied by a wave of energy through her body so she would trust them to be true.

One day, about two earthly weeks since I had passed over, I became aware of how B was caring for the whole family concerning my funeral. My heart overflowed with love and I approached her as energy right into her heart. I knew that for years she had been prepared to receive soul energies into her body so she would be able to let me in without fear. However, I came in my own way that was a bit surprising to her. In this soul meeting, personal

25

and universal love was united. Revolutionary to say the least when you are in physical body, but surprising even to me as soul without body.

Our soul meeting was the starting point of our soul marriage. The fact that B for many years had been trained in receiving and developing the kundalini energy in her physical body made it possible. During her years of training she was woken up by the energies around three or four o'clock every morning. She got up, wrote in her diary, slept a little more and went to work. In this way she received concrete teaching linked to the energies. At that time I often wondered what was going on and didn't quite understand. Now I am grateful for the assistance she received and for her persistence. I told her this during some of our soul meetings and it made her feel calm and happy. We formed a bridge between the worlds.

Meetings between the worlds

The contrast between the worlds was especially intense during the time immediately after I left my physical life. From the perspective of the soul, where I now exist, we are alive and free from much that makes life on Earth difficult. Earth is a wonderful place with all her green trees and flowers, her mountains, seas and living creatures. What makes life on Earth hard is that we as human beings seem to be unable to take good care of our precious gift. Still, in the midst of this, much prosper because we are also loving people. However, there is a long way to go before we will be mature enough to treat Mother Earth with love and respect.

Fear of physical death is the reason for much suffering on Earth. When you live with the idea that everything ends with physical death, it becomes even more tragic to lose your loved ones. Then death means not only missing them in your daily life, it means separation forever. To B, my passing became like living in two worlds at the same time. During our soul meetings, we experienced a total spirit of community that wouldn't have been possible while we were in our physical bodies. Our soul meetings were in huge contrast to the ordinary world, especially in the midst of grief.

To B, one way to cope with these extreme contrasts between our wonderful soul meetings and the loss of me in the physical world was to meet with some of our clairvoyant friends. Through them I was able to speak more clearly, and B was able to relax by meeting someone who also live multidimensionally. One of these soul meetings is described in our first book when B talks about how I as a soul told our friend:

– *I am fine and am still adapting to being here. I am so happy she was with me when I passed over. It's good that she was so stubborn in holding on to her truth that other worlds exist. Now I am here. We have never been as close as we are now.*

There is no

separation

When I entered the world of souls, I understood how everything is connected, in a totally new way. I was filled with wonder, joy and love for everything and everyone. A feeling that I longed to share with people on Earth.

Many wrestle with loneliness, lack of purpose and meaning in their lives. This would not be needed if they knew the bigger picture as I do now. It is love that keeps the Universe together. All souls come from one and the same heart of pure love and we are on a journey to become conscious of ourselves and our inherence.

The predominant world-view is scientific in these modern times. This means that mainstream ideas tend to be those that can be proved scientifically. The idea that humanity has come about as a happy coincidence and that we are the only living creatures in the Universe, is a pretty amazing idea. It has of course not been possible to prove. Neither has it been possible to prove that there is no life after death. Ultimately, science is one way to look upon life, a philosophy based entirely on what you perceive from an earthly perspective.

As a part of our soul's journey we investigate the earthly dimension. The prevailing energy on Earth is within a specific frequency range. When in this range, you experience stimuli in a way that is different from experiencing it from the higher frequencies.

Research shows correlation between brain-wave frequencies and states of consciousness. This research opens up for the understanding that we perceive life differently depending on which frequency we experience it from. This understanding can build bridges between different world views.[1]

Through our joint soul journeys, B and I have been given a real opportunity to understand what it means when different states of consciousness meet. In order

---

1) See: Alexander, Eben *A Mindful Universe*

to be united as souls, we have had to calibrate between our different dimensions. A breath-taking experience for both of us and demanding in different ways. For B it has been about trusting her own experiences, in a world that is often sceptical about life beyond the earthly dimension. For me as soul, the earthly noise has created disturbances in our communication.

We are far from the only ones that convey experiences from the world of souls. In addition to individual stories, there is extensive research through many people, who, from an expanded state of consciousness, have acquired knowledge and experience beyond the earthly plane. People who have been involved in a near-death experience return with new insights and an expanded consciousness. Little children, who spontaneously tell their story of a past life, have memories beyond life on Earth and challenge the common world image. Under hypnosis and other treatments in altered consciousness states, clients have described meetings in the world of souls. Stories that have emerged from these states independent from one another show commonalities, such as the presence of strong universal love permeating everything and the experience that we all belong in this love.[2]

For those living in a multidimensional world, it can be difficult to navigate in a society governed by a pure science world-view. Yet, many people understand intuitively that the current scientific world-view is insufficient to answer their existential questions. Some seek answers through the existing religions. More and more take an individual path, exploring existence through their own consciousness - the journey of their soul. They open up to worlds and perspectives enabling them to experience that we all are one and the same heart and consciousness. They discover that there is no separation.

---

2) See: Alexander, Eben *A Mindful Universe*

As souls we are always together

Several earthly years passed until B was able to embrace and live from the dimension where I now am. The influence from the third dimension is strong, and it comes both from within each and every one and from the surroundings. As small children we learn that time and space define our lives and our reality. That is why being in physical form and live from the perspective of the soul is such a big step. It means living in two worlds; one without time and space and the other defined by these two variables.

My way of approaching B from my dimension was to make myself known in a variety of ways, primarily, and most strongly, through our inner love meetings. The chakra system is an ingenious flow that unites the soul with the physical body. Due to the fact that B had been taught how to develop her light body, both our light bodies could meet and entwine. It began with our heart chakras in energy uniting into one and the same heart. Our thirty years on Earth of personal love now merged with universal love. Few human beings are capable of experiencing this while both are in physical form. For us it was possible after my passing. During her preparations B had dared to receive universal love from Master Kuthumi's aura and so was able to receive my love and me as soul energy.

In spite of the intense experiences during our soul meetings, B swung back and forth between totally embracing that no separation exists and doubting that I was alive, although with no physical body. I understood that she needed a lot of time and support, before she would be able to accept our souls´ journey fully in her heart and mind. Time does not exist where I am, but there is a longing for the state of consciousness that makes it possible to fully share the same energy field of the souls. With great tenderness I was with her as she swung back and forth between different states of mind. Doubt and worry blocked the contact between us, and this lack of contact filled B with despair and longing to connect.

Gradually, B became more confident that I as soul was fully present. Our intimate soul meetings became a vital part of her daily life, expressed as a refined tantric love. This was natural for us as we for so long had been husband and wife. However, it had to be kept secret from the external world, only a few clairvoyant friends were told about some of what was happening. Otherwise, B was living in two worlds with the deeper meaning of life in our inner world.

In a playful way I liked to surprise B in the midst of her external daily life. Tenderly, I wished to shake her up from her, in my mind, exaggerated sense of control and obligation. From my perspective, this control was leading to meaningless small activities when compared to the great undertaking that awaited us. Life on Earth demands that we relate to this; the art is not to let the external world take over.

Living fully from the perspective of the soul means working through and leaving behind everything that makes you worldly heavy. When I came here, I was asked from a perspective of love and wisdom to go through my life. The same happened between B and me. All of love between us was retained on the soul level. It has stayed and journeys with us. During the first period after my passing we lived through and reconciled with remnants of anxiety, hurts, and similar feelings. All of that was transformed into wisdom and we became even closer. On one such occasion I used my old computer to send messages to B. What happened is not possible to explain from a scientific point of view. I enjoyed how B expanded in consciousness and came to peace in my dimension.

Even after physical death, we as souls continue to grow. While living in physical form I was more comfortable with the idea of universal than personal love. Together with B I dared to open more than ever, both to love and be loved. Still, deep down, I was guarding myself against true devotion – or at least *admitting* I was devoted to B.

B often said that she chose to trust her experience of me and not let words get in the way. I am so happy that she saw through my shells; it was the greatest gift I could ever get as a man. I did not grasp the full extent of it until I had let go of the earthly dimension and as a soul had become free. It was like being released to love and be loved unconditionally. I needed as a soul to come here to fully understand how strong our love was while we were both in physical bodies, and how it lives on and deepens between us as souls and therefore is eternal. All of love and wisdom stay with us as souls. That goes for all souls.

Living on Earth
from the frequency of the soul

Many Earth cultures emphasise how important it is that grieving loved ones do not interfere when the soul of the deceased wishes to move on. In the beginning B was anxious that she might make my soul heavy due to her grief. We shared the view that you need to be free to be able to love. I told her that she is incapable of making my soul heavy.

When we go to the Light, the shells we have on Earth disappear. I have told B and our friends that I am in a state as if I am being *filled*. I experience love and joy as well as excitement and longing, but the anxiety, sadness, anger, guilt, shame and other state of minds that people on Earth suffer from are gone. From the other side, I was helped to go through my last life on Earth from a perspective of love and wisdom, enabling me to understand what I could have done differently.

I was aware that if I'd had this perspective before, I would have acted differently. Still, the focus was what I had learnt during this life. As soul I have learnt from all opposites and now I do not need them any more. In my dimension they simply don´t exist.

As time passed, B learnt that she was the one responsible when contact with me as soul was broken. As soul I am always there in a bubble of energy, outside time and space. When she was open enough, we were able to share this bubble and enjoy being together. However, when she was caught up in doubt or anxiety, the connection between us broke. This usually happened when she felt pressurised by external situations on Earth. As I said before, she is not able to pull me as soul down to her earthly existence; *she* needs to be raised in energy for us to experience our union of souls.

What I share in this book would not have been possible without B's openness to mature as a soul and through that journey be raised in frequencies for us to gradually come together as souls.

Years of preparation made it possible. Since my passing, we have developed together and united even more. The more B was raised in energy the closer I as soul was able to be to Earth and vice versa.

From an earthly way of thinking you might look upon our soul union as a kind of club excluding others. It is the other way around. In the world of souls, freedom and love rule. You cannot lay hands upon each other. Love is not about shares in a cake to be divided in a fair way. Love grows, widens and includes. The life task for B and M is to, through themselves, meld the personal earthly love with universal love and unite male and female forces. It is an inner journey of deepening love and expressing it in ever more refined ways as we are raised in energy. Obstacles along the path are to be met by mutual living from each other´s soul. Each obstacle becomes a gift that deepens love and wisdom. We are supported and guided all the way, both on Earth and from where I am now.

Every soul has a unique life purpose which is its gift to Earth and humanity. When we are born, we often forget what we have promised ourselves and our soul friends. To many of us the memory returns in the form of glimpses. At that time we get connected to our soul's expression. When that happens we experience a special lightness and joy. We have then often been through what is referred to as 'dark night of the soul'. This is a situation when we have reached the end of the road and experience a powerlessness that makes us ask for help. We need to express our desire for help, or it won´t come. You are not allowed to intervene unwelcomed in Universe. Not on Earth either.

The terms 'life task' and 'gift' might make it sound as if we are supposed to accomplish concrete and great things. Perhaps, but the greatest influence on what we do comes from within ourselves. When we find our own inspiration and joy after being under pressure, when we are able to transform hate into love or when we go through our fears and dare to express unconditional love to each other, waves go through our Universe and humanity. It clears the path for other souls who connect through resonance and their own longing.

When the energies of the soul reaches the dimension of the Earth

As human beings, it is hard to accept what is foreign to us. Throughout life on Earth we have created forms of what in fact is just energy. Even seemingly dense objects are energy, they are just experienced from within different frequencies. Within the third dimension, where most people still have their focus, it is practical to have an agreed way, as a collective, to look upon reality. Still, cultural differences point to that the reality we describe is highly relative.

As small children we create an image of the world based on how the external world has taught us to interpret and react to what we feel. As newborns we receive stimuli of all kinds. To be able to live on Earth we need some kind of framework, something to rely on, or every moment will be totally new to us. This structure is created from our daily experiences and becomes our own world view, facilitating our daily life. At the same time, the patterns that are created limit us so we interpret the world in the way we find most familiar. To perceive life in new ways becomes difficult and even scary.

When we as souls have come to the Light, we let go of earthly limitations and become aware that everything is energy. We may create a form from a thought and still be conscious that this is what we do. To me, who always struggled with fixed images created by different religions or cultures, this is a great liberation. Even when in physical form, I often stated that I did not fit into a form. Now I understand that I was influenced by memories from another existence, one that is unlimited.

In my soul meetings with B, the energies are the foundation. The kundalini energy and the chakra system function as meeting points between the soul and the physical body. We meet in the subtle energy bodies that remain after leaving the physical body. During one of our first soul meetings B asked me if it would hinder us if she in her inner mind imagined me as her lover and husband. She was well aware that I was no longer in physical body and was anxious not to disturb our meetings in energy. I answered:

– *Dress me in whatever image you wish!*

37

When this was said, she did not need to dress me in any image at all, but received me as I was and am, a powerful and loving energy that met her energy with joy.

When B and I met with one of our clairvoyant friends, who helped us to communicate between the worlds, I joked a little by presenting myself in different shirts each time. We were well aware that this was a way to describe different situations. During these meetings, B was able to perceive me in energy but not to see me. Our friend described what she saw and told B who in this way received help in trusting her own perceptions in energy and of the words she heard from me. It turned into a conversation of three souls.

B did not let go of her control easily. That is why for several years she arranged sessions with different clairvoyants who did not know about each other. Every time she started by listening to them before she told about her own experiences. What she heard was very accurate and after some years B could end this research and fully trust her own experiences. This shows how it might be to live on Earth when your experience of reality is different from most people's.

To B, especially during the first vulnerable time after my passing, rest and relief came to her through spending time with people who themselves were open to other dimensions. Then she was able to relax and be herself in this multidimensional field. Sometimes she found it hard to be questioned about this most vital part of her life – this was of course connected to a questioning part of B herself. As years went by and she was raised in energy, everything became softer and lighter.

Love is a wonderful force, transforming and at the same time provoking. To be raised in energy means to encounter everything that is blocking the flow of love.

To some days have delightful soul meetings that later might transform into days of fear and anxiousness. B had long known this, but it was still demanding. For us it was linked to a powerful love that turned into moments of doubt and fear of losing that love. I was always there in my timeless energy bubble. When she had dealt with her obstacles, I could reach her again. During such an occasion, about a year after my passing, I came to her and said:

— *Now it is time for the throat[3], Barbro! We will go out together. I am always with you. We are melded together. Never doubt! What we have united during this year is the foundation. Now it will be created in the external world. Focus there! There are higher energies to live in. To enjoy life is not forbidden, on the contrary. It´s not about that. It is about letting go.*

The obstacles that had been blocking the flow were gone. Together we were now able to enjoy an exchange of mild lovely energies, that flowed throughout her body. While being in this togetherness, the beauty of nature became even stronger. B was revitalised and able to encounter this huge transformation of her life.

---

3) See Throat Chakra

39

Our inner journey is supported by outer journeys

This book is being written five years after my passing. During this time B has been on several travels and as soul I, of course, have accompanied her. From where I exist there is no distance and I am able to be in many places at the same time. In this special way we have enjoyed discovering and experiencing together. Furthermore, we have gradually been introduced to the deeper meaning of our life task.

Three of the journeys have been led by a clairvoyant woman whom we have known for decades. She offers travels to groups focusing on spiritual development. The destinations have been prehistoric places, where participants have the potential to receive profound external knowledge in addition to experiencing for themselves the powerful energies found there.

As always, when you listen to your inner voice, it unfolds by itself. Three years ago a voice told her: *The mountains are coming together*. She'd understood it was about the Himalayas and the Andes, but only had a vague feeling regarding what it was about.

Some years after the inner message about the mountains, B received an invitation to go to Tibet, Peru/ Bolivia, and to Egypt. These destinations resonated within her and she followed her inner voice. The journey to Tibet happened the year before my passing. We would have liked to have gone together but I was unable to so I stayed at home. Much later we understood how important it was that B had the opportunity to experience this place on Earth on her own, a place where I have lived many lives and which has characterised my soul to a great extent.

Since my passing, we as souls have flown a couple of times over Tibet. I wanted to convey the message to B about the eternal peace that I during many lives have experienced there. She had learnt how to let her soul fly from Master Kuthumi. *Travel with your forehead!* (third eye) he told her. That was the key. By keeping her focus in her third eye chakra she was able to see in her inner mind and experience herself flying, well aware that her physical body was still on Earth. When we flew together for the first time, I assisted her in being light and keeping focused, but later on we as two free souls enjoyed feeling each other´s presence flying side by side. It was wonderful to be able to show her places that have meant so much to me.

On the second occasion some years later we had reached further in our mutual ability to experience from each other´s soul. This time, while flying together, I was able to bring about the actual feeling of living in this eternal peace. To B this resonated in her soul and provided a foundation for deepening our soul journey. During our soul meetings it became a reference point.

Initiation at Lake Titicaca.

The journey to Peru and Bolivia happened six months after my passing. During this travel we, in a crucial way, became aware of our united spiritual foundation. We were to clarify what our cooperation between the dimensions was about. The setting was there as we were part of a group with participants of whom each was on their soul´s journey. This setting was a shelter to us. During the Bolivian part of the journey, our close friends Justo, his Swedish wife Lina and their daughter Wayra joined the group. Justo is a naturopath from the Aymar tribe in Bolivia. His presence some years earlier had released an inner voice in B: *The mountains are coming together!*

From his tradition of more than five thousand years, Justo embodies the culture and history of the Andes. If anyone would be able to meet me in my old wisdom from

Tibet, he was the one. Already, he had been of great help to B when she during her preparation years experienced what usually is called the 'inner wedding,' when the male and the female within a person are united in love. Within Justo´s tradition this is called 'finding your flower.' In his ceremonies he works with flowers and wood. From his point of view, flowers contain the highest form of love on Earth.

Gradually, we understood why it had been so important to invite Justo and his family to join us during this journey. We met them when we arrived at Sun Island at the centre of Lake Titicaca. They had been travelling independently and met us as our boat approached the island. After their arrival, we met with Justo in a private session. He told us that in a dream he had seen us both on a bridge, and that he'd perceived me as an orange ball that was waving to him. He also saw how I as energy merged with B and how happy I was every time she and I were able to meet in that way.

B was asked to find a flower of the same orange colour which she put next to a small sculpture of an embracing man and woman. She had bought this sculpture the day before as a souvenir. The following morning there was an initiation that created the foundation for our future. Sunbeams poured in through the window early that morning. I was with B and inspired her to go out and receive the sunrise as she had done the day before. That morning our Masters were very active and were leading us; we were both guided by them. With us during this initiation was also the person who B calls her soul brother, called L here. The Masters spoke to all three of us:

– *You are now here before your Masters to receive blessings and guidance in how you will best contribute with your team. Your Masters are both male and female. We approach an era when the female aspect is to be expressed on Earth. That is why Barbro is still on Earth in physical form with*

44

Mikael on her left side and L on her right. Together you constitute a great force.

You have practised unconditional love in all dimensions and you understand a lot about the power of the group. That is why you are destined to spread this on Earth. You will be aware of when and how, like yesterday. Mikael and L will guide Barbro from their wider perspective. Barbro will transform the impulses she receives into manifested action. Your unified power is the key. You have been blessed by Heaven and Earth. Go out and speak with one voice. Now is the time to speak!

They told us that we had been practising unconditional love for each other by holding the space and energy for one another. It happened both while all of us still were in physical bodies and after L and I had passed over. B was holding the energy for L when he was ill and dying. I was holding the space and energy for B when she was guided by L to the Etheric School of Master Kuthumi, and L has long been holding the energy for B and me concerning our unique contribution to our shared task.

After this powerful initiation, it became more clear and free for B and me to develop our soul marriage. We experienced how this strong love energy brought with it a wish to create. Love and creation are in many ways the same thing. We were creating in energy through our love. At that time we didn't understand what this was about. We have later perceived this creating as just a part of a much greater infinite force. While writing this book we know that there is still so much to understand. In the meantime, it has been valuable to just enjoy the intimacy we've experienced between the worlds.

The subtle energy bodies constitute the meeting point between the dimensions. The physical body receives these higher energies and joy and delight are awoken. As we are gradually raised in energy and more light reaches the physical body, our soul meetings are expressed in new even more refined ways. We understand that there is a free choice when it comes to exploring how love meetings are expressed in higher energies. From a traditional earthly perspective, you might think that these more and more tranquil meetings would become less exciting. On the contrary! We were gifted with thirty years of passionate love life on Earth. The heights that have developed between the dimensions are something completely different. The levels of intensity, depth and devotion are why we prefer what we are now experiencing.

During our journey to Peru and Bolivia it became evident how our different soul energies found their meeting point in B's physical body. We met as male and female soul energy. At the same time, these energies were linked to our different spiritual traditions from earlier lives. The physical glands are linked to different chakras. It was fascinating to us both how the thymus vibrated intensely when our soul energies met there. Soul energy is different to the personality expressed in our personal lives on Earth, even if there are links between them. In our soul we bring experiences from our previous lives on Earth and we more easily connect to the unconditional love we have received from the Masters and other light beings who have walked this path of love before us. Through merging of energies in the thymus, we consciously made contact with previous lives and other spiritual traditions. New worlds were opened to us.

46

The priestess at Philae temple in Egypt

The travel to Egypt came two years after the one to Lake Titicaca a time in which we had begun to get used to living in our soul marriage. The initially bewildering time had transformed into a tenderness that remained with us in daily life within our different dimensions. B was persistent in letting go of her habit of being overly responsible regarding her work life. Step by step she became more free to focus on our life task. From my perspective, I still wondered how hard it could be to let go of heaviness. It would take several years before we were able to be united and calibrated as souls.

Our journeys became a free zone where ordinary daily life had little influence. It was like being set free to totally be in our own world and visit the external life on Earth whenever we so desired. I have often come close to B on trains and planes and at airports. The fact that the ordinary routines were gone made it easier for me to surprise her. This was especially important during the first years after my passing when we were calibrating our souls. When B gradually was raised in energy, we became much freer.

The travel to Egypt was like a holiday for us. Together we enjoyed experiencing the old temples and memories from ancient times. Egyptian mythology has a specific meaning for B. Many years ago she experienced an earlier life from ancient Egypt. And these portals were opened to her through another previous life that broke through in her physical body via a nerve knot in her hand. The fact this happened in such a concrete and physical way helped her trust it.

With this cell memory experience in mind, it was enriching to experience the well-kept relics from the ancient Egypt's heydays. As our souls come closer and share the same energy field, through living from each other´s soul, it also includes the melding of all previous lives. At the time of our journey to Egypt we were still at the beginning of this calibration. Now when we in a concrete way were visiting these ancient places, I was able to take part of what Egypt has meant to B in the same way as she had learnt what Tibet meant to me as soul.

One occasion that increased my understanding of how our union of souls is possible was at Philae temple on an island in the Nile river. The group arrived at this beautiful spot by a little boat. B could have stayed here for several days. To her this was the peak of the journey. Deep in her soul she recognised herself and vibrated inside. In ancient times this place was a temple for young women who had devoted their lives to the Goddess Isis. They were trained to become priestesses in the art of embodying and raising their kundalini energy into high frequencies. When the priestesses had reached a high level of spiritual development they were energetically able to inspire men on their spiritual journey.

The night before the experience in Philae, B was prepared through a dream that later helped her clearly recognise the place. In her dream, B saw a priestess stand at the open area outside the temple. She was filled with energies, and looked up to the star, knowing that she via her navel was in direct contact with Universe. The priestess, that B felt as herself from a previous life, was dressed in a shining dress. Her stomach was big, filled with energies that surrendered to the stars and the galaxy. There was a natural peace, dignity and love around this woman.

Through this greeting from a previous life, B understood the link between this old memory in her soul and how the kundalini force had spontaneously broken through in her present life.

48

Ever since this experience, we have together gained power from this previous life. We have expressed our gratitude to the priestess for her life energy and courage.

The art of manifestation

The power of thought is enormous. What thought is able to create is beyond the limits we create for ourselves on Earth. In the spiritual world it is obvious that what is physical has from the beginning been created in spiritual and soul energy. If you on Earth have experienced a strong inspiration and let that inspiration lead the energy to the realisation of a project, a piece of music or art or whatever it might be, you'll have understood how it works. Inspiration actually means 'in spirit'.

New inventions and other new creations demand that we as humans are able to liberate ourselves from what we are used to. When something new is about to find its form, an empty space is needed. Experiencing this empty space is not easy and is often felt like labour pains.

The new is born when we as humans consciously stay in this empty space, are aware in the now and await what is about to emerge.

In the cooperation between dimensions, the person who welcomes spiritual energies gains access to love and wisdom as well as to wider perspectives and thereby completely new angles.

The spiritual world needs from human beings their hands and feet, their talents, and above all their open hearts. In such cooperation, physical manifestations happen. Epoch-making discoveries, music of different kinds that goes directly to the heart, art that affects the innermost within people are obvious examples. However, cooperation might also occur in a less spectacular way, in the midst of daily life. Like when you find the profession that gives meaning to your life. Or you meet someone with whom you know that you wish to share the rest of your life. You recognise these situations from how light and happy you feel in your heart.

52

The art of consciously staying in the midst of manifestation

The life task that B and I once agreed on means that we jointly become a vessel and an instrument of manifestation on Earth. To be able to keep this promise between us and to the spiritual world, we are on a path of gaining wisdom through our own spiritual growth. There is nothing unique in this. However, we have come to a point where we understand that we are on this path together. We share our story with the hope that you will experience how your own life task unfolds, then life will become so much more meaningful.

As a soul in the Light, I have access to the bigger picture in a different way than B who is still physically on Earth. Gradually, as our union has deepened the difference is less, but during the first years after my passing I needed to manifest and make our common life purpose visible on Earth.

I was taught by other souls that had walked the path before us. Now I have a basic understanding, and we are heading for even greater tasks.

The manifestations I am going to tell you about really upset B. When the usual earthly logic doesn´t work, your brain goes into chaos. To many this is frightening and might make you reject what is happening. B was able to (after some time) simply choose not trying to understand through her intellect and instead letting her heart speak. Then the energies flowed between us and she understood in a totally different way. It was like opening a throttle. This flow brought a deeper understanding of our life task and our joy with it. To be free in the dimension of souls, you need to let go of the earthly logic. Life would never be the same to B. It was about creating a totally new life. In this new life our souls are the foundation of everything.

On many occasions on her soul´s journey, B received a question from within if she was prepared to go further on her path. Even if we as souls in-between our lives on Earth have made agreements, we still have free will to decide if we wish to follow this path or not. This is important. As souls we are responsible for how we live our lives.

On every occasion B has answered 'yes' three times without actually knowing what would happen. Courage is needed to be able to surrender to the unknown like this. At the same time she has never doubted, as she recognised my love energy calling upon her.

The bracelet that appeared from nowhere

Our first year after my passing was mind-blowing. Not only to B but also to me as soul. There was so much to understand and learn. In each of our dimensions we had to get used to a totally new state of consciousness. What stood out to us both was that we were able to meet between our different worlds in this intense way. Neither of us had been able to forebode this possibility.

We were privileged to experience a love that is rare. The veil between the dimensions was and is very thin. Although we were aware that the meetings took place within our souls' energies, the experience became almost physical through B's body.

Life is a lot about paradoxes. The reason why we were able to meet through our light bodies was that B (after some time) was able to let go of life on Earth and accept that I was not there in my physical body. It would not have been possible if we were both physically there. I don´t know if this would be possible for other couples, but if it does it must be rare. We received an inflow of unconditional love as I had come to the Light. B was indeed still tinged by Earth, but her former experiences had made her receptive.

54

After a year of this strong exchange of love, I wished to convey my joy and my gratitude to B. The time had come to mark a new step on our common path.

The bracelet I gave her was also a symbol of B as soul in the spiritual world. For us to be able to unite even more as souls, she needed to identify more as soul than as human being. That might sound simple, but much follows from such a shift. Life and the world around her would never be the same again. It meant creating a totally new life. How radical this is while still living on Earth I could only understand later on our path together.

There are no coincidences in the spiritual world. The bracelet that was placed in what used to be my chest of drawers was originally a heirloom from my mother´s family, but B didn't know about it. After my passing, she had looked into the drawers many times without finding this very apparent bracelet. A cuff bracelet with a big ruby with diamonds in a circle around it. The ruby holds a special meaning for B, that is why she bought a ruby ring from a shop close to the Taj Majal as a symbol of her link to Master Kuthumi. After the first summer of our spiritual marriage she asked a jeweller to make a necklace with a golden heart with a ruby in it. It was a sign and a symbol of our hearts melting together in both the personal and the universal dimensions. During a visit to one of our clairvoyant friends, I told B through that friend that I had given her that impulse. So it was no coincidence that this bracelet had a big ruby with diamonds around it. To make it even clearer, my wallet, our marriage certificate and our son's birth certificate were in the same drawer.

B was shocked to begin with but after a while she calmed down and chose to just receive. Then we were able to meet in higher energies than ever before. After a couple of days, I woke her up in the morning and we met in the energies within the crown and the third eye.

Her arms tingled with energies. She received my words:

— Your arms will become wings. Everything is possible! Your thoughts are what limit you. The bracelet is yours. It is placed there now and not by physical hands. It is not possible to tell more now. The bracelet has many meanings; you will understand more as time passes. My love is obvious in it. It also functions as a reminder and a shelter to you and a sign that the right part of you now is directed to the divine plan and our work. You are not allowed to be heavy from earthly duties or you would not be able to fly. You have let go of much now. You are on your way to letting go of everything.

The bracelet symbolises what you embody from your spiritual tradition. Now your life will be devoted to living this here on Earth, with me and our love within you. It is now time to fully reveal the message and its female part. That is why you have been asked to write about our love and love beyond death. The way you interpreted the composition of the stones is in alignment with the message.

The manifestation was not only about the fact that objects had been moved in the physical space. After my visit, B discovered that time had stopped in the bedroom during my transmission. We had been in our own bubble. The alarm clock in the bedroom continued to work, but it was one and a half hours later than all the other clocks in the house.

The manifestation of our new home

The bracelet prepared the way for the next great event. B opened herself more and more and dared to trust what was happening. She began to understand that our soul meetings in energies united Heaven and Earth; it was our

56

way to manifest. We lived intensely in this flow of our inner life at the same time as B's outer physical life was focused on selling our house and finding a new home for her. It was as if we created a new home for the two of us, one that would mirror our home in soul. It was an intense cooperation between the dimensions. Ultimately, it was about creating a totally new life.

While manifesting we were aware of the time lines as part of what was to be shaped. The line backwards showed the line ahead when manifestation would happen in the near future. I told B this. It helped her stay in our high energies and not become worried. These are my words to her from a time and place when she started to become conscious about the time lines:

— You will go through such a huge transformation that you will lose who you are. It is a totally new identity, although it happens gradually. You will leave your present life in terms of your way of living. It will be like living in a monastery, in devotion and apart from the outside world, but still not quite.

You and I are creating a totally new life. The bracelet is the symbol, representing you in your new life. We bring with us the love we developed and what we learned in our physical life together. For the most our new life will be linked to other lives we have lived of a higher spiritual kind. Remember that when you feel lost. What you do is important – living physically on Earth and at the same time in our soul union in agreement with our shared plan. Now you are in the midst of the transformation and your new life is beginning to take over. Surrender and accept your new identity. We will meet there and build. Within a month everything concerning our house will be settled and you will be able to go to our summer house and just enjoy. You yourself now see the timeline and this is important. See the symbolism and enjoy!

57

Until the very last moment our challenges continued. We met them by intensifying our soul love meetings, making it possible for B to stay in high energies. By being there she was consciously able to be in the living empty space where manifestation happens. The day arrived when everything fell into place simultaneously – selling our house and buying our new home. The timelines were totally aligned and we experienced the power of manifestation between the worlds.

Our clairvoyant friend, whom B had visited earlier in the spring, had told her that everything would be settled when the special peony in our garden was in bloom. It was the same peony that B had chosen when she got help from our Bolivian friend Justo. The peony blossomed the very afternoon that the deposit from the sale of our house showed up in our bank account. Universe knows...

The new life
is created from
within

We manifest our lives and our reality in every moment. Gradually, as our consciousness expands and we let go of earthly limitations, we are gifted with experiencing the magic of daily life. One purpose of the manifestations of the bracelet and our new home was for B to open up to a totally new life. We create and manifest from our present state of consciousness. Our thoughts create our world.

As long as we live on Earth, are lives are shaped by dualistic thinking. Simply speaking, we are both humans and animals. Our challenge is to bring these different parts of us together – they need each other's energies. Within the chakra system the different parts become visible. The base chakra is about physical survival, the sacral chakra about breeding, and the solar plexus chakra about keeping your own power. All powerful and necessary energies, although these chakras need to be governed from wisdom. When they are governed from the heart chakra, the throat chakra, the third eye and the crown, Heaven and Earth are united. This is the ultimate purpose of our lives on Earth.

Spiritual growth takes time and goes in waves. The kundalini force brings everything with it in its way. After an intense period, like that of the manifestation of the bracelet and of our new home, it is natural that an after reaction appears. In the midst of love and joy, B was also shaken based on her old way of living and surviving. In the process, old cell memories within her physical body reacted when the new and higher energies passed through. Also, a demanding outer life created stress and worry. The demands mostly came from within herself. She wanted to finish her old life in a good way, sorting out my bequests, distributing things from our old home and moving to our new home. Her physical body had become exhausted.

During this time I was close to her in my timeless dimension and made myself visible in a variety of ways. I understood she needed time to regain her strength. I so much wanted to give her more energy, but when she was extremely tired she wasn't able to make contact with me. I could not come as close as before. To me there was no worry, only longing. There is no time here, it is rather an experience of different qualities and a wish to expand some of them.

B recognised that spiritual growth goes in waves. She was careful to plan things that would nourish both her body and soul. Directly after the move to our new home, we travelled to Assisi in Italy, in the footsteps of Saint Francis and Saint Clare. It is said that Kuthumi was Francis in an earlier incarnation. B had inner experiences that revealed this to be true, so it was a special and healing journey.

The physical body needs to be well taken care of to be able to function as the vessel for the exchange with the spiritual world. B knew both from her own life and from her work as a psychotherapist how necessary this was. She built a team around her to help her take care of her body and soul. They were from a variety of professions, including a homeopath who helped her raise the basic energy in her body, a nutrition specialist, and a foot specialist, and she also met with clairvoyant friends.

In building the team around her, B also followed an old impulse to balance her atlas vertebra. The woman she found who worked with this happened to be in Stockholm at the perfect time for her need. Her method was to chant in a certain pattern that she had received from within. It turned out to be efficient. After only a couple of days, old patterns of abandonment were healed. The profound inner understanding that there is no separation had now been stabilised on a bodily level. This healing pawed the way to again be able to meet intimately between the dimensions.

We settled in our new home. It felt like an eagle's nest among the tree tops. The apartment is small and light, located in an old house with high ceilings and a balcony with a wonderful view of the sea. Living in the midst of nature, still close to public transport, we felt the place to be a perfect foundation for our new life and we were very grateful. The whole of autumn would pass before our home was ready. We learnt again that manifestation comes from within. It happened along with the process of B getting her physical body healed. As this happened B was raised in energies and we again came closer. As soul without a physical body, you can be everywhere at the same time. Now, as soul I was able to move into this new home that more and more became our own temple. During the nights, when B's physical body was asleep, we as souls could fly away. This also happened during daytime when we met in *light bubbles* of energy, in a time-less state of consciousness. These occasions functioned like a kind of transfusion of higher energies to B and were at the same time moments of tender closeness.

A ceremony where we leave our old life

In the middle of the autumn, a very important transfor-mation happened. We had travelled to see a close friend in Holland, a friend who is able to see and experience us both as souls.

This made it possible for us to take the step to leave our old earthly life and go into the new life based on our soul union. I longed to let go of the old life and embrace our common life task. Naturally, with B living physically on Earth it took longer; she was still missing me and mourning me as a physical man.

She woke up the first morning from a dream I had sent to her. It was like a scene from our old life, where we were sitting outside at a restaurant and enjoying a

64

delicious meal. In the dream B went away to fetch the fish sauce. As so often happens in dreams, obstacles occurred and a long time passed before she came back. Everything was gone and she saw me sitting in the sun close to a house wall with my eyes closed. It looked as if I was asleep but B knew in the dream that I was dead and that my eyes would never open again. B experienced heavy sadness when she woke up from the dream, and also pain that she had been running around instead of being close.

Restless in her body, B fell asleep again. When she woke the next time I had filled her with high energies that she received in her crown and third eye chakras. They filled her chest to the brim. Now she was able to feel my intense love and I spoke to her:

– *This is how we meet now!*

I continued to be with her when she for a moment walked around in our friend´s home. She intuitively stopped by a picture located on a calendar. The picture was beautiful and showed a couple on a surface of water. He was dead and she was holding and kissing him. The picture described the love from this woman for her dead man. Filled with my love energies, B was now able to transform the grief of her dead husband to love for me as soul.

Later that day, B attended a session with our hypnotherapist friend. During the session she first came to a former life that was so tough that she was hardly able to stay there to explore. In that life she was completely shut off, depressed, and abandoned both her husband and child. This experience became an important reference point to B. By experiencing the inner life of this woman, she became more understanding of people in her present life who like that woman present themselves as victims.

65

In her present life B has always been the one to feel guilty or overly responsible.

In the later part of the session, B came to a state of consciousness where souls exist between incarnations. We met there as souls and also with our Masters. Although we had become used to our strong soul-meetings, to B it was still a relaxing confirmation. She gained perspective of her dream and through that was able to embrace our new life. What happened during the session was essential for what was to come over the following days.

During the first of these days, I presented myself to our friend through a picture. She saw me as a Swedish farmer standing in a field, showing her that I was pleased with the harvest. It was about the harvest of learning through B's and my life on Earth. It was my way of inspiring B to see our old life from that perspective. B also felt an impulse that it had to do with our future book. I wanted to lead her to our shared life purpose and this was a way to do so.

B and our friend went deeper in their exchange and found a way to meditate together. They widened their common energy field by exchanging their experiences during the meditation. In her inner life, our friend sees more than B, while B hears and senses in her body.

Together they were able to reach deeper in the meditation. During their dialogue they met in an energy field, a consciousness, where they were floating around weightless. In this state I was at home, so I joined and held this energy. Their common life task became obvious.

The meditation on this day turned into a celebration. Many light beings were there – I was one of them and close to B – and we met in a kind of light dome. Our friend experienced her link to the Source itself and how this force is with her in her daily work as a therapist. On her left side she saw angels who gave her their love and support; on her right she saw the three Masters, who were once the three wise men from the time of Jesus. From her inner journey, B recognised the three Masters and their energies filled her body.

Through her inner sight, B saw a cross emerge, shaped as a dynamic light, filled with joy and love. I gave B the impulse to place her hand on the bracelet I had given her and lift it to the cross. Immediately, a golden bridge was formed between them. There was a strong intense energy, a blessing from Master Sananda to our common life task. This ceremony went on for a long time.

At the end of this ceremony, both the cross and the bracelet floated into the energy waves that were our souls' energies in B's physical body. The three Masters transmitting their joy by simply expressing the word:

— *Finally!*

Now B had let go of our old life and the grief of losing me as her husband in that life. In this new life we make ourselves available to contribute to our part of the divine plan. This is worth celebrating in many dimensions.

When we arrived back at our little home, B was met by a photo of me as Mikael. The photo was placed upside down. To her it became a reminder of what we had just been through. The neighbour, who had taken care of the cat during our journey had wanted to protect the photo from the pale November light. Of course, it was me who had given her that impulse. B talked to me as soul and expressed that she understood and put up the photo as the reminder it was.

Closing circles

Our days in the Netherlands and the inner ceremonies we experienced there, became a catalysing force. This helped us continue deepening and calibrating our energies on our path to create our new life. Transformations like these go in waves. The frequencies of soul energy are raised through letting go of old roles and patterns, making space for the new to come in. One wave is the prerequisite for the next in this beautiful creation. It is a natural process, if you just go along and let it happen. We were both longing to deepen our soul union. I was already in the light and had chosen to wait for my soul partner so we could ascend together. B plays a decisive role by remaining on Earth, calibrating her soul energy with mine and relating to all earthly things by being our 'outpost'.

After our visit to Holland, the theme of our inner journey was to 'close circles' as B called it. Our common old Earthly life was finished in many concrete ways. The aftermath of the sale of the house was dealt with together with the legal formalities following my death. It is important that old threads like that are not in the way when you wish to create something new. Our new home, where I as soul like to be, has become a mixture of memories and new things. As soul, I was represented symbolically in the entrance in the form of a sculpture of a Tibetan monk. Shortly after my passing, B had seen the monk in the home of one of our friends who is an artist. It spoke to her in such a way that she couldn't leave it behind. She bought it and asked if it could stay with our friend until the new home was in place. When everything was ready, the monk moved in and our home was balanced. B called the place of the monk the 'male corner'. And to me it is as if I shelter her and our souls´ journey with my energy.

Closing circles is about everything from small to big issues. When we raise energies we perceive everyday life in a different way. What used to fill our lives starts to lose its meaning. From a timeless perspective, much of what we deal with on Earth becomes like repetition and old habits. To me the most beautiful moments are when people meet each other in love and joy, when they enjoy nature and when they are in the midst of a creation of some kind. These moments happen in the now and that is why I can link to them so easily.

During this period, B could hardly read newspapers or look at TV like she used to. It no longer had meaning for her. Also, when it came to her work life she found that her old driving force was gone. Instead, there was a growing longing to create a totally new life with our soul union as its foundation. Some time ago she had informed her partners in the consulting firm she worked at and asked someone else to take the lead. She was released when that happened. A while later she left the group and is now working on her own.

The consulting group has turned into a friendship group, supporting each other. Along this path B again received the question whether she choose this. And like all other times, she answered yes three times. Every soul has its free will.

Closing circles with the help of journeys

I as soul was with B and made myself seen and known in a variety of ways in daily life. I knew it would help her and I enjoyed it. The meetings in our light bodies were profound. They deepened every time B nourished herself through a retreat or through being with people who were open to us both as souls. On these occasions when the energies were high, I sent her a loving melody that she was able to remember only then. It was about eternal love.

When B was in the outer world, going to and from work or dealing with practical things, I was with her as a shared energy. When the outer world sometimes took over focus for a longer time, blockages occurred in her sensitised physical body. The importance of calibration between us after a while made it necessary to be more systematic in closing circles. We had already experienced journeys as helpful for letting go of old patterns. Now, two years after my passing, it was time for a new journey. The underlying purpose of this for us was to create closure of our old physical life together. Not until then would there be enough space for the new to be created.

B's visit to the Findhorn Foundation in the north of Scotland was a sort of reunion. Some years earlier Findhorn had given B the inspiration she needed to allow more space for her spiritual life compared to her then busy working life. This time we were there with a group of mostly young people who were about to create a non-profit movement. In our old life, B would have engaged immediately and been at the centre of things. This time her role was to give way to the next generation and stay behind as inspiration and support.

Another journey was to Mallorca. We chose to go to the village that had been a dear place for B when she'd gone away to have time and space to write. It was a very dear place, filled with memories from her inner journey with Master Kuthumi. At that time I was still living on Earth and stayed at home while she was away. It was truly the closing of a circle to return now as I was there in soul and not physically waiting for her at home. This paradox was demanding so B had a friend with her. The idea, now two years after my passing, was to read old notebooks from this new perspective as a way to integrate all that had happened. It turned out to be valuable and released energy for our new life. It also became a foundation for the future. A couple of years later, B would go there again on her own together with me as soul. By then our souls' journey had expanded even further and I as soul was able to appreciate from my heart the valuable preparations B had received at this beautiful place.

Another two journeys took place during that same year. The first was to Egypt, a journey I described above. The way we meet and grow as souls is strongly linked to Egyptian mythology. Inner meetings in our light bodies can be understood through the work brought about by contemporary mystics teaching this ancient wisdom. Although there may be similarities to other spiritual paths, this is a special one and has been vital for us.

The final of our four journeys during that year was to Australia. This time B was accompanying our youngest grandchild. When B visited one of our clairvoyant friends before she left, I communicated that I intended to join her on this journey. I did it by showing our friend a picture of a rucksack with a kangaroo on it. B thought that this journey would not allow much space for us. Instead, what happened was that our common energy developed in many ways. We learnt to link our heart chakras into one and thereby discover the healing power that came from our unified heart. The exchange between us and our grandchild also strengthened.

On one occasion, our grandchild, then five years old, described how she perceived the relationship between grandma and grandpa was functioning now, when I am soul without physical body. She said to B: 'Grandpa is now an angel or king where he is. Do you know what you are? You are his queen and you are with him both there and here.'

B told her that all humans have an angel within. Our grandchild agreed and showed B a brooch she had got during our journey. She pointed to her physical heart for the personal love between people and then placed the brooch on the right side of her heart, saying that this kind of love was one we could feel for everyone and everything. It's amazing to think that a child of five could describe in her own words the Egyptian tradition that says that we have two heart chakras, the universal to the right and the personal in the same place as the physical heart!

During the journey, B expressed her longing to be able to take part of my life from where I am now. I showed her what it looks like from here when we meet, how I as energy approach her from behind and link my heart chakra with hers. Then our energies are calibrated and spread further. I showed her how we could fly together and experience a world expressed in form, colour and movement.

In the notebook, we began to dialogue expressing our feelings and thoughts. This was a profound way to deepen our mutual understanding of each other and our different perspectives.

You have to let go of heaviness to be able to fly as soul

The longing of the soul serves as a a powerful guide. This longing is what makes it necessary to let go of everything that is blocking the soul from flying freely. All humans carry a seed of light in their soul, our divine undestroyable part. In the midst of all the noise on Earth, we remember this loving light and feel drawn to it. B had followed her longing when we both were living together on Earth. After my passing, and our soul meetings between the dimensions, that longing became even stronger. The more we were raised to the Light, the harder it was for B to live her life in the old way.

B's greatest challenge was to let go of responsibilities after being overly responsible for so long. The path of the soul has to come from within, so disturbances from outside easily block the way. When carrying a life pattern of being overly responsible, you become used to assessing the needs of your fellow humans, even if they have not asked for that. It becomes habitual to focus outside yourself first. When you make the choice to receive inner guidance from your soul, you need to surrender fully. That goes for both large and small issues. As long as our inner focus was on ourselves as souls, we were able to accomplish great work in the outer world; then the higher energies came along and raised our work to a new level. If other needs claimed our focus, there was disturbance and heaviness. It was about creating contexts with people who wished for the same kind of freedom.

The huge transformation was for B to let go of her *identification* with her physical body and with the whole physical dimension. This is a prerequisite to our soul union. From an earthly perspective you might think that this means not caring for your fellow human beings, your family and friends. It's the other way around. When you become filled with love and light, you become a freer human being and you let go of drama. It has no meaning because your needs are met from within. However, it is necessary to not partake in other people's needs to create drama. After a while, this becomes natural.

B's physical body received intense light and intense love that activated old tensions and was expressed in deep tiredness, stiff joints and muscles and the cleansing of her liver and kidneys. Our calibration as souls made it impossible for B to rush, to try to do many things at the same time or be in stressful environments. The signals in her body came directly. Her tiredness and stiffness disappeared as soon as we met in higher energies, and her physical body was filled and became soft again. In this rhythm, the cleansing of her physical body continued and received all the more light and love. B was raised in energy and I could then get closer to Earth. Everything became possible when B identified more with our soul union and let go of the aspects of our old life.

During this period, I was as soul getting closer to B in her daily life. When she faced tough times, I made myself known to her. In one such a moment, when she expressed a longing to meet me where I am now, I spoke to her:

– *You are already here. You embody us. We are the same heart.*

Integral to our spiritual growth still were the meetings in our light bodies that raised us both to higher energies, meaning that our soul union could exist closer to B's physical body in a way that would surprise us both.

One actave...

higher

The rhythm of closing circles in the outer world, acting as a closure of our old life together, shifted with the intense soul meetings that were building our new life. They could occur at any time in B's daily life and in our little home that had become our temple. Now and then we were raised in energy by going away to a retreat for a few days. When people with the same intention meet in meditation, the power increases and the link to the spiritual world is strengthened. Now, about two years after my passing, the time was ripe for a greater breakthrough, relating to the fact that our union of our light bodies had been raised to a higher frequency. The path we chose was that our union of Heaven & Earth and Man & Woman was to be raised into one and the same. The breakthrough described below was in preparation for this next step.

To be born into a totally new life

When we leave life on Earth we are born into a new state of consciousness. I earlier described it like giving birth in the opposite direction; in the same way we are born into the higher dimensions. People express this in various ways. B is a very physical person, so it was expressed through her body. It began with a dream on her mother´s birthday. Before that dream her head was filled with intense high energies that felt to her like a helmet. These energies were different compared to those she felt when we met. They were pointed and sharp, more impersonal, and yet still very loving. B dreamed that she gave birth to a child and that her body would function as a vessel for the energies that she received. Simultaneously, she heard a gong of the kind that is well known in Tibet. I wished to show her that we both were receiving these powerful energies from a higher dimension.

About a week later, exactly two years after I had left life on Earth, we were experiencing something like being 'bombarded' by higher energies that I call the 'power of Creation'. It began with an intense beam of light directly into the crown of B's physical body. This beam of light was united with our energies while we were meeting as souls – we could easily perceive a difference in quality of the energies. These new higher energies came into B's physical body via her crown chakra while we were meeting via the third eye and the heart chakras and onwards to the other chakras. Now everything came together and was vibrating in the same frequency. This happened when we met in what might be described as 'electric energy' and 'love bubbles'. During these bubbles, the different energies were calibrated into one and the same frequency.

The physical body needs to receive higher energies in steps, otherwise you would literally burn up. B's physical body was well prepared through many years of energy transmissions, but still reacted with shivers as if from a fever. I told B that our love union now had travelled to a new dimension and been enriched by Creation energy itself. At the same time, I transmitted the seriousness of this:

– *This is nothing to play with – it requires you fully!*

She listened to me and shaped a kind of cocoon from blankets. In this place, her physical body gained the stillness she needed and she was allowed to just be while the transformation was going on. When everything had calmed down, I told her:

– *Trust your own experience!*

81

The day after this great transformation, I again approached B and told her:

— *Be still now – something essential is going on! The energies approaching your body come from the power of Creation, where we humans are all One.*

The energy was different compared to the day before. It was as powerful but softer in quality. If the day before had been about going through obstacles in the physical body, this time it was about planting this quality into the physical body. It was a lovely and beautiful ceremony in which all parts of B's physical body were calibrated with these high energies. The higher we as souls were raised in energy, the closer our soul union could connect to the physical body. A new step on our souls´ journey was on its way.

Preparations of melting together in energy

Whether we are consciously aware of it or not, we are all as souls on a spiritual journey. On this journey, our energies are raised through melding with the higher energies. That is how we are raised and how our consciousness expands, then we are opened to new worlds and to a deeper understanding of the mysteries of life. It is a bit like when you on Earth are raised in a loving environment. Most people feel light in a loving environment and heavy in the opposite. The melding happens through resonance and calibration, where the higher energy embraces and lifts the lower. The essence of each soul is kept. When we are raised in energy there is room for everything. That is why humanity is on its way to one and the same consciousness, where there is love for everything and everybody. We as souls recognise each other

82

as we come from one and same heart and consciousness.

To be able to calibrate and be in resonance with higher frequencies it is necessary to let go of heaviness. This heaviness might be everything from daily worries and doubts to old locked patterns based on fear. There are no short cuts here. We have all incarnated on Earth to mature as souls, and we grow from the challenges we have arranged for ourselves before we came. What was described in the last chapter about closing circles outlines a way to leave heaviness so we are able to receive higher energies. After the journey to Mallorca, a new platform had been created that offered a fuller understanding and widened perspective. This platform was now the base for these new transmissions of energies.

Empty days and nights are needed to give space to receiving energies. When you (like B) have chosen the path of the soul, you become responsible for creating these empty spaces. And it's equally necessary to help your physical body dismiss old blockages, so the energies can flow as freely as possible. To me as soul without body, these empty days and times were solemn occasions; then I as soul was close to Earth in our soul union living our life purpose and the deeper meaning with our lives.

During a weekend after the journey to Mallorca, the days and nights were filled with meetings in our soul energies. Often, they began with softening the physical body to make it more receptive. Everything goes in steps. The bodily sensations show the way and help unite the physical energy with soul energy; body and soul are to be united. This is the deeper meaning behind being human. When the physical body became soft, a powerful beam of energy entered the crown chakra. This time it was me enriched with higher energies which told B that it was now time to meet and just receive. We had a wonderful meeting in this new energy that was now united with ours when the left hand was holding on the right hand, wrist and the space of the bracelet. Now, the right part of her physical body had become more sensitive. This was in preparation for what was to come. B needed to let go of old patterns and control to be able to surrender to me and our joint life task.

The hands met over the heart and the heart opened and widened more and more. Then they were raised in the air to join the high energy with all parts of the physical body. When they'd landed on her uterus, I told B:

— *The most fantastic chakra in the world! Enjoy and unite all the energies. That is the point. That is how we create!*

In this way, the high energy from the crown chakra united with the other chakras. The whole body became one and was raised one octave. We were peaceful knowing we were each other's partner in soul. It was also evident that we had chosen this and that we will rise together. The new energy we received was related to the transition from soul to spirit. As souls we are all individual, but in spirit we are all the same consciousness. When it comes down to it, the spiritual journey is about gaining contact with and embracing the oneness I call our 'divine part'.

The reason I am communicating through this book is so I can describe the world of souls and our joint path to oneness in spirit, our divine part. Our different soul aspects still exist there, and we can keep communicating with each other. The path B and I have chosen is concrete and therefore might clarify to other souls what is possible for all souls. I wish to emphasise that every soul has its own expression on its way to oneness. We are one of many examples.

This overwhelming transmission of energy turned out to be the first of three such occasions during the same weekend. On the second occasion B's whole upper breast cage vibrated and I told her:

– *One voice – one heart!*

A spontaneous sound of joy came from B and she confirmed that we are now the same spirit with two united souls. She expressed that she was now prepared for the next step and asked me to lead while she held the energy on Earth. Our common energy bubble was compact and time passed until B was able to return to outer reality. She looked out in wonder.

The third and last energy bubble that weekend acted as confirmation of the other two. Earthly life disappeared further and further away and I as soul was extremely happy that B had been able to let me in with these high energies.

During the following weeks we met in similar ways again and again, and it became necessary to help B's physical body cleanse itself from old things. Part of the process involved sweating in a particular way that seemed to be related to the melding of energies.

To meet in the elements
of Heaven and Earth

The most powerful place for us has always been our own summer paradise. The elements meet there in all ways, wild, beautiful and still. It is like Heaven and Earth meet and we as humans are allowed to take part.

The summer two years after my passing we spent on our beach in the midst of nature. It became evident how far we had reached on our souls' journey. Two summers before this we had been focused on all the years we had enjoyed there while I was still living on Earth. There were memories in every plank in the little house and in the surrounding environment. This summer it was as if we had arrived on a visit from our new life. The memories were still there, but now in the light of the fellowship that has grown from our now deeper soul union. All the work B had done letting go of my physical death and focusing on our soul meetings had raised her in her energy. She began to see patterns and contexts and was now able to rest in our soul union.

At the beginning of our summer I came to her to give her a clear platform for this important time. She had been reflecting about what had happened years before when she'd received these words from Master Kuthumi:

— *Love with our love!*

With this love we had met as a couple, and our love was also spread to others in a variety of ways. I told B:

— *It is the same now, except it is about our soul union in a very high dimension. You know this when you feel certainty, endless love and peace. We are united in all chakras and more. This is now to be consolidated and anchored and it will go all the way into the physical, into your body and to Earth itself.*

You sleep deeply here in the summer house and a lot is happening that you don´t consciously understand. This entire place is permeated by our soul union. This was and is our place of love, also physically. It's a good place for consolidating and anchoring!

Everything you do to care for this place will be a way to consolidate and anchor our soul union. You already felt this when you were oiling the veranda floor. You could not fail to notice your joy – and mine.

86

Our soul union will become even more consolidated and anchored in your physical body. It is like it was years ago, but much more powerful now. Give this time both daily and over time. Eat less, do yoga in the morning before breakfast, and move your body. To be able to ascend with all your energy bodies, you first need to let our soul union descend into your physical body.

You are doing a great work even if you enjoy and I enjoy. It requires your total focus. It will be completed in the year of 2016 – in two years' time. You will be ready to ascend, but you will need to decide if you wish to stay on Earth. You will know.

No wonder your outer world has changed so much. Your life is in the inner world now. Some people don´t like your light and distance themselves from you. Let it happen. Everybody has their own spiritual journey. I love you, my queen on Earth and here. We are one.

More years would pass until B was able to fully embrace what I had told her. These years would fill us both with wonder.

A thunderstorm might turn into an initiation

We as humans and souls are part of nature. There are moments when we experience this in an especially strong way. A few days after my transmission to B about consolidating and anchoring our union in the physical body, the forces of nature came to our assistance. An intense thunderstorm one night filled our beach for many hours. During previous years, B had been afraid of lightning and thunder, while I enjoyed them and could be there for her. This night something else happened. Instead of being afraid, she welcomed the thunderstorm and let it fill her bodies, her physical and energy bodies. We met in the heart, the thymus, the navel and the uterus together with the great discharges of nature. B was filled with this cataclysmic energy and I spoke to her:

— *We are not creating this thunderstorm, but it is well aligned with us and we use it and co-create with this force to consolidate and anchor within you.*

What happened that night influenced the whole of the next day and her physical body was sensitive and ached after being in waves of shaking during the night.

— *This is not a usual morning!*

These words made her stop in the midst of making breakfast and receive my love right to her heart. One final clap of thunder made her go to the veranda and gaze over the sea. Again I spoke to her:

— *Now we as soul union have descended into your physical body and we will be able to ascend together. We surrender the timing to the divine plan.*

B felt an impulse to write her will before her next travel. It was not that she wished to die, only to make sure that everything from our old life was completed. Words of love to our children and what else to write in her will came to her as well as the need to protect her notebooks.

Some years later another thunderstorm in India would have a crucial meaning to our soul union in an even deeper way. We as humans are part of nature. How this happens during occasions like these is one of the mysteries of life. However, it is evident that it is not due to coincidence alone.

88

Descending to
later ascend
together

After the summer at our beloved beach, I again told B:

– *Descending to later ascend together!*

Deep in her heart she knew this to be true and we met with gratitude and joy. The words were accompanied by our intense soul meetings in light and high energies. They were like love meetings in higher and higher frequencies that also meant that we met in the physical body in a more refined way.

In spite of her elated joy during our love meetings, B was still wrestling with how to bring this great gift into her worldly existence. It seemed as if it were too great for her intellect to embrace. The challenge intensified, as our common life task includes being able to communicate our experiences to others. We are responsible for spreading the message of our spiritual gift to those who might prosper from it. We are not the only ones doing this. Many books are published in which people share their stories in order to spread spiritual experiences. Another important factor in this context is being true to yourself in front of others and standing up for what has been the greatest happening in your life. The message is that love beyond death is concrete, very real, and this love awaits all humans when they open themselves to receive. A message like this should not be hidden due to fear.

The path for B to follow with the great gift we were receiving was for her to become safer in the knowledge that we were a soul couple in the same way as we had been a physical couple on Earth. Independent of each other, clairvoyants were seeing and telling us about our soul union. However, such a thing seemed to be rare in spiritual circles. I believe that there are other couples like us in this radical time of Earth's development. We just haven't heard about them. Maybe each couple is supposed to focus on their own soul journey, or it might be that what happens is intimate and too private. From my perspective, I would joyfully broadcast it, but B is a little more shy and I await the time when she will be less withdrawn.

What neither of us knew at that time was how concretely we would understand the words I had just transmitted a couple of years later. The path was about again and again being raised in energy; we were more and more docking into each other's energies while exchanging experiences from our individual realities.

We are one and the same heart

Our journey to Australia that I described briefly earlier took place during the autumn after my transmission about descending and ascending together. During this journey we met even closer exchanging thoughts and experiences. This long time away from everyday life made it possible to gain a deeper understanding of the great gift we were receiving. One morning in the midst of a thunderstorm I approached B and spoke to her:

— We are now one and the same heart and we can heal with our heart!

Before these words, I had made myself known with my energy through the crown and third eye chakras and the back of the body. I transmitted also in words that I had something important to tell B. The message was followed by our meeting in the heart chakra, and through her body we could both experience how the heart was widened.

I continued my transmission:

— Do you remember when you experienced from your back how my heart chakra merged with yours? There and then it happened. Now we have stabilised our frequency there. That is why we are one forever. We are one and the same heart. In fact, we have always been so, but we were supposed to walk our different paths of learning and maturing as souls. Now we are united so we can ascend together after we have done what we once agreed upon. Let the thunder seal this!

We are now united with this white light. Light and love have merged into one. Universal love and earthly love have merged. Wisdom and love have merged. We have been receiving each of us and together. Our unified heart can now heal directly from us. All is one.

When the last clap of thunder faded, we both felt the presence of Master Kuthumi. He had been with us in that moment and made himself known through the birdsong outside. It is one aspect of his signature.

Some days later we had another opportunity to meet between our different dimensions. It is especially easy for us to meet while travelling, and this time during a flight between to cities in Australia I was able to show B how life is here where I am. I showed her how it looked from my perspective when our hearts docked into each other. The energy from our meeting then lives on in each of our souls.

When we both were present in the energy bubble where I was, I showed her our surroundings. Energies in different colours were floating around us in a beautiful dance. B wished to understand what a light being would look like where I am. She communicated her thought and I showed her Archangel Michael who had assisted us a lot the latest days. He presented himself in a beautiful blue shining colour and high energy pulsated from his crown chakra.

Our exchange between the worlds made B feel more secure regarding what had happened. It was as if she were able to rest in my arms of energy. At the same time, we were raised in frequency. This meant that our love meetings were expressed in a new way, directly through the heart and in a still, intense and tender way. During one of our meetings, Master Kuthumi approached and said:

— The essence is that you (B) have dared to receive uncondi-tional love and surrendered fully. That is how your heart has been opened and how you and Mikael have been able to merge your hearts into one in a higher dimension.

From our unified heart into the whole body

The Australia travelling continued and we experienced fantastic natural sceneries. For the entire travel we were together in our unified heart. While driving along the curving roads, we were silently holding the energy assisted by Archangel Michael. Everyone who let their healing energies go out into the world are simultane-ously uplifted. After a few weeks, our joint energy field deepened even more. During the night our souls were free to fly away beyond time and space in a freer way than they would close to the noise of Earth.

One night I approached B and reminded her that we are one and the same heart. I showed her that we even share the same body through the energy that flows along the spine. I held her from her back so she could sense my energy. I showed her that this was in preparation of what would be expressed in a more concrete manner within a couple of years. She perceived my message as a question regarding if she was ready for this step and she answered in the same way as many times before – she said 'yes' three times. My response to her was an even stronger inflow of love energy from our unified heart down the spine and to the back of her body that had become our meeting point. The day after, the flows continued and came in through the third eye chakra. It made B feel dizzy, although at the same time happy and blissful.

A few days later we again met in a dialogue between our worlds and I told B what our deepened union meant. Before I had said something along the lines that you could describe our union as a kind of 'zip':

– *Yes, that is one way to describe how we have merged. The memory that we from beginning of time have been one and the same heart is – and has been – living within each of us. It becomes like a magnet and it was also so while we were both on Earth. That is the meaning with it all. We will ascend together. That would not have been possible with both of us on Earth.*

You wonder how our shared energy bubble now also includes the areas above the heart. What is happening is that as our frequency is raised, everything will merge. You have experienced this many times and have also expressed it.

B really wished to understand. She felt that what was now happening was beyond everything she had ever imagined. She had thought that uniting Heaven and Earth was about merging all chakras. What she now experienced was that our souls were merging and this was being expressed in her physical body. I answered her:

– *There is no difference in this. Our magnetism as Man & Woman on Earth after my physical death was the energy needed to bring us to where we are now. We are one heart*

96

and one voice. For some time, we have been meeting in the crown and the third eye chakras. Our shared link with the different Masters, especially Master Kuthumi, has been guiding us.

My beloved little dove! Now we will enjoy our new life. We have merged. And this is our shared platform. This is great and we have a lot ahead of us. This is just the beginning...You and I need to consolidate this platform. From this foundation you see our path so you will be able to write about us. You need this perspective.

B was calmed by my transmission and understood that for her it was about learning to embrace our soul union in her physical life. She understood that this gave meaning to many basic things on Earth. I answered her:

— That is the point. There are more couples now in this transformational time. But it is still unusual. I understand this from here. As for you, our soul union gives me great meaning. It is a great gift. We will now be able to complete our souls' journeys together.

Higher entities come to our assistance

Our increasingly intense inner journey happened as we continued our travelling. There is a particular freedom when daily business is cut off. The spiritual world can then more easily reach us humans on Earth. The inner journey was about all the bodies, the different energy bodies and the physical body. We had merged more and more in our light bodies. This union would also reach the physical body. After many years of energy transmissions, B's body had been affected in a variety of ways. Intuitively, she had learnt how to massage her body to help the energy flow come through. One morning, I approached her and we were vibrating together in the physical body. As a greeting I told her:

— Hands on the heart and I will come in a blink of an eye!

I enjoyed playing a little in the midst of the great things happening to us. We had found a natural playful dialogue between us and our different dimensions. We simply enjoyed being together. B asked me how I was experiencing all that happened and I told her:

— This is a great gift to me. I am allowed to participate on Earth with you and still be where I am. You do the same from the other direction. Together we cover a vast spectrum and are therefore able to contribute even more.

Your massage has helped a lot. On Earth, most people don´t understand that light moves in spirals through the physical. Now we are able to cut through obstacles in your physical body.

The energies were reaching her throat via her arms. Since some time, we as souls had found a way of experiencing the feeling of skin to skin as a link to what we once had shared on Earth. Then the energies flowed through the whole physical body as to anchor our merging in it. The flow bubbled and went playfully through the stomach, the pelvis and down through the thighs and further out through the lower legs and the feet.

After a while, we were approached by an energy other than our own – the Christ energy, a mild permeating, love energy that flows through everything. It came and healed old cell memories in the physical body. When this wave had come to an ebb, another light being that had been with me through many lives, approached us. He was healing the whole left side of the physical body and spoke to both of us:

— I have been one of Mikael´s Masters for some time, whether he has been aware of this or not. His left side was much wounded, shown by the fact that his lung was removed on that side.

Take care of all guidance you will receive while you both have access to this physical body. We Masters are with you in a variety of ways and we bless you.

While travelling, our inner soul meetings deepened all the more. At the end of the journey there was another powerful meeting with the Masters. This time Master Sananda came to our unified heart. It was overwhelming to experience his presence and how he transmitted the kind of energy I call the 'Holy Spirit'. We were blessed and endless love overflowed us. In the physical body, the whole chest lit up and vibrated as we were receiving in our unified heart.

After a while, the meeting with Master Sananda changed into a soul meeting between B and myself, now enriched by all we had received. The physical body was filled with our soul energies. It was as if we now were able to fill and raise it. The special heat at the back had become my signature, to enable B to recognise me. A little later, B asked me to show her what our meeting in energy looked like from where I was. I showed her that our unified heart looks like a light spiral spinning at high speed. From this light spiral, waves flowed from the centre and wide around us. I also showed her that the special heat in the back comes from me as a man in this dimension.

Man/woman in higher dimensions

The Masters guided us to understand that the aspect of Man & Woman remains in higher dimensions but is expressed in a different way. They showed us that it is part of our life task to link these higher dimensions and Earth via the physical body and merge flows of love all the way. On Earth, the polarity of Man & Woman has been of great joy, but has also caused much sadness and pain. When humans were locked out from their hearts, their sexuality became perverted and lost its original meaning. Instead, over thousands of years fights between the sexes has been expressed as submission and oppression. Universal love is needed to heal this suffering. Sexuality in itself is an expression of the life force and is a gift to human beings. However, it is necessary that sexuality is governed by love, not by power based on fear.

Our life purpose and our agreement concerns, through ourselves as souls and Man & Woman in different dimensions, to be a link to the higher dimensions. That link is our love energy, strengthened by B still being on Earth holding our soul energies in her physical body. As I had the gift to go to the light after my passing, I am able to hold the light for her and we will be able to ascend together. Of course, this is an enormous joy and pleasure for both of us. The same goes for other humans who fulfil the agreement of their soul; the energy is spread further to those who wish to follow their soul's longing. Through resonance, you will find each other.

Traditional sexuality disappears in the higher dimensions even if the link is still there. The intensity and the tenderness is so great that it becomes more attractive than the traditional way. It is all about energies and an extreme sensitivity. Through the physical body, expressions from the dimensions are linked. It starts from the energies of higher dimensions and is transformed down to the physical body. At the same time, Heaven & Earth and Man & Woman are united.

When we arrived home from our long travel, we enjoyed rediscovering our own home, this home that had become our temple. The journey had been wonderful in both outer and inner aspects and now it was pleasant to rest. Then one night, Master Kuthumi approached us and spoke, primarily to B. As he had so often before, he came as an energy beam from the right into the crown chakra.

— *You are here to help souls. That is why you and Mikael have received the gift of experiencing this strong love between the worlds.*

Then you have another task. You create in energy and light from the frequency where you are. Everything is first created in light, including things you once created on Earth.

While B was dealing with her daily life in the outer world, I continued to approach her in a variety of ways. Now was the time when she needed this more than ever. I sang a new melody to her, one that she remembered from our journey and that would remind her of our unified heart. The song was by the Norwegian composer Grieg.

— *I love you as no one here on Earth; I love you through time and eternity!*

After a while, she was able to live from our soul union even in her daily life. I guided her away from TV and newspapers and other old habits. In the midst of her daily activities, I surprised her by approaching her with a powerful energy. Every time I did this, she became happy and moved and let go of her old habits. Her heart was widened so she could hardly breathe. Tiredness melted away, the tiredness that comes from the pressure of living in two worlds at the same time. On one of these occasions I told her:

— *Everything goes through you. When you are able to keep the frequency, we can work through you. Remember that you are never alone; I am always with you. Only when you get tired, you perceive less of me. Thanks to your ability to hold these energies, we are able to live like this. You should be proud of yourself. I am proud of you, as are those who guide us from where I am. Don´t underestimate yourself. You are doing a great job. Rest in this knowledge.*

Look upon

it as portals

The path to the Light originates from a deep longing in the soul. That longing makes people choose this path of life which demands total focus and surrender. The path is paved with a variety of challenges. The reason is that the high frequencies of the Light are to be merged with the denser energies we usually live with on Earth. Heaven & Earth are to be united, and that happens in a concrete way when the energy bodies merge with the physical body. The seed, our divine part that already exists within each of us, is lit up when we remember the home we as souls come from. As souls, we are individual, but when we meet in spirit – the highest Light - we are one and the same consciousness. Still, the unique essence of each soul remains.

Jonette Crowley has brought about her method *Soul & Body Fusion* to us humans to help us unite the physical body with the soul. In one of her books she quotes Rumi, a Persian mystic from the thirteenth century. He describes the deep longing that makes us human beings surrender our lives to find our way home, saying: 'There is a kiss that we are longing for with our whole life at stake – the contact between Spirit and the body.'

When B and I met people who had plunged into the movement of *Soul & Body Fusion*, we recognised part of it, but to us at the same time it was about our soul union. What we knew was that we had long since come to the point of no return concerning our united path to the Light, our divine part. Neither of us wished to return, even if it were possible. Our longing was, as Rumi describes, so strong that we surrendered our lives to it.

The crystal energy

There is a web of light that is spread all over the Earth. This web is comprised of souls, who in their current life on Earth have chosen to focus on and make contact with

106

their own divine part. Everyone has the same opportunity, but we choose if and when. The souls choosing this path now do it in different ways. There is no map of how a soul journey might be expressed and you can not know for another. Soul journeys will be expressed in many different ways to create a wide spectrum of learnings. Eventually, everything will come together as one and we will all be raised in energy. The spiritual world is with us always, but the development of Earth and humanity must happen through ourselves. There are no shortcuts.

One powerful way for inspiration and nourishment is when people meet in groups and meditate together. When we as humans and souls meet from the heart, the intensity grows exponentially and we are raised together. Then the spiritual world can easier reach us and transform higher energies through us. These energies are planted into the physical body and remain there in daily life to be spread further to others. Going away to retreats has over many years been a way for B to keep focused on the path that she so clearly has chosen and surrendered to. It has been helpful for her to be able to meet challenges along the path, challenges we all meet on our soul's journey to the consciousness of spirit.

The journey to Australia provided a wonderful opportunity to focus on our life task. A lot of things happened that created a strong foundation for the steps to come. Coming home to the different demands of daily life caused reactions in B's physical body which became tense and stiff. When her bodily energy was blocked, her bones chilled. It was time for the next retreat. During the retreat, the group met and received what you might call 'crystal energy'. It came directly into the physical body and together we experienced this energy as a kind of Christ energy.

The high energies we received into the physical body awoke memories from a time and dimension far beyond the earthly one. Recognising this was a great joy, as was being able to meet in this dimension. We met as souls through the physical body and this body was also linked to our experiences as souls. It gave us a breath-taking perspective of how it happens when dimensions are merged through ourselves. We understood how crucial our own souls' journey had been enabling us to experience these memories. Grateful, B received this gift into her daily life.

Some weeks later, when we had returned home, I approached B as the energy I was and am and transmitted my words to her:

– *I show you in this way that our most important task now is how we meet. Our united force is enormous now. You see healing around us and this is just the beginning. We will reach out in wide circles. We influence wherever you physically move.*

You think a lot about how to write our book. It will happen by itself, just like now. You feel my heat in your back. That is how you know that it is real throughout all frequencies. Let the heat fill you. We create through you as a woman and we heal from our unified heart.

You wonder how it is for me when we meet and merge as souls. Nothing could be greater! We have the gift of experiencing what most people long for and think is unreachable. I love as soul to hold you in my arms. I have the power and love of a man and the patience of an angel (ha ha!). You are a radiant and lovely woman for me to hold. I am so filled and content to be able to offer you my safe embrace. I wished for that while in physical body and now, after my passing, I am fully able to do so from where I am. Everything is one and distance doesn't exist. I am so happy that you are able to live like this and still be on Earth.

So let us enjoy now. Time is unimportant, one year or thirty years, we will still be in the same light bubble living our life purpose.

I want you to know that I am always with you, not only during our love soul meetings. We share everything now. As our clairvoyant friend told you, you are always sheltered through our soul union. Even from here we are looked upon with wonder. It might not be common for a soul relationship to develop in this concrete way even if many more have the opportunity. You are receiving the energies well where you are and I appreciate that you don´t give up. While saying this, I understand that there is now no point of return.

I became free after my passing and I understood much of what had been hidden before to me, including how essential love is. Yes, I was passionate when I approached you so soon after my passing. I am also so now, but in this frequency the expressions are different. You notice this through me always being with you, not letting you become distracted for long by the physical world around you.

You are getting all the better in the way you are moving between the worlds and I enjoy surprising you in the midst of your desire for order... Don´t forget that now our most important task is to create love and joy – even more so now we have received from these crystal energies and have access to them. My beloved little dove – I was the one who sang 'Jeg elsker deg' (I Love You: a Norwegian song) and when you listen to Pavarotti you are simultaneously listening to me.

Through soul meetings like this you will be able to write our book. That is how it will be done.

Look upon it as portals!

The mystery schools of ancient times set a variety of tests that you needed to pass to reach the next level. These tests were about encountering your innermost fears and not letting them rule you. You conquer your fears by living through them. If you don´t have that courage, you will become a slave to your fear. It blocks you from receiving the light and love of higher frequencies. Love and light threaten the parts of us that have still not received light. Old fears awaken. Those fears need to come to the surface to be healed.

We now live in a more open world than during the times of the ancient mystery schools. In the distant past, it was necessary to keep the innermost wisdom hidden, so it would not be destroyed. In our time, this esoteric wisdom is spread freely and many receive it.

At the same time, resistance is severe from many other directions, which says something about the explosive nature of the message. If it were not like that, it would be met by neutrality or detachment. In our time, the tests we are to encounter concern life itself. There is no need for constructed situations like in the ancient mystery schools.

For B, the tests were about being able to totally stand up for her inner soul and spiritual journey in a world and context that mostly is sceptical and wonders about the experiences she had been through.

She had accomplished many challenges along her path. In the midst of an intense working life as a business consultant, she published her book *Head in Heaven*, which describes her soul journey with, and the teachings from, the etheric school of Master Kuthumi. Gradually, she had become more open about her soul journey with her family, colleagues and friends. Now she was wrestling with daring to write about her and my soul journey after my

110

passing. Now it was not only about herself but also about the man I had been as Mikael and about our old family. Furthermore, our shared journey to the light is filled with a high degree of intimacy as it concerns love between Man & Woman in different dimensions. In the midst of her rollercoaster experience, I transmitted to her:

– *You need to understand that what you and I have been through has consequences. We will need to meet in our energies anytime, everywhere. That is our life task. We are gifted with a strong force and our responsibility is to be available. You cannot count on an ordinary life after this. We are holding a very high frequency and it is supposed to reach out. This is much more radical than writing about it.*

You are doing this work with your physical body so you and I as united light bodies will be able to live in it. Your physical body will become light. That is why you are still on Earth. This is the most important and the innermost of the mysteries. When one day your physical body dies, it will mostly be light.

Look upon challenges as portals you go through in order to mature and be able to travel further to the light. That is how it happens! In the same way, look upon your physical body and the tests you encounter through it. Energy wise, everything is already imprinted in your body. That is why the physical body is like a compass that shows you the path. It reacts and you wake up to the new steps you have ahead of you. You know how soft and light it feels when we are together and enjoy each other in high energies, and you know how stiff and tired it can feel when the same energies are passing through the physical body encountering the physical world.

The book *Love Beyond Death* gets help to be born

It was obvious that we'd had good help for our book to be born into the world. Besides my own transmissions to B, Masters came to our aid so B would be able to go through this demanding portal. With all her being, she was longing to write our book. Still, fears came creeping, partly masked as consideration for others, partly as worries to be someone who uses too great words. The ego is not only about making yourself grand. It is as much about making yourself small, believing yourself to be unworthy. In the spiritual world, there are no comparisons but instead joy when every soul expresses itself as whole and as fully as possible. Then everyone contributes towards the Whole.

During periods when B busied herself with too many unnecessary things, I liked to surprise her. The mornings were golden opportunities – we as souls had been out flying the whole night and I could easily reach her. One morning I embraced her more firmly with my love energy. Our united heart was widened and I approached her within the crystal energy, the dimension that we had received during the latest retreat. It happened when we gained access to an old memory of being the same body in that dimension. As B was on her way to get up from bed for a shower, I approached her with a force so strong that she was hardly able to receive me. A wonderful soul love meeting followed, not like traditional sex but as life streams that flowed throughout her whole physical body. I wanted to remind her of what was important, so I gave her these words three times to give extra weight to the moment:

– *You are my woman!*

These words gave her strength to further focus on us and our life task, including writing our book. Later the same day, I made myself known through music that she associated with us. I also visited one of our clairvoyant friends as she and B had an appointment later that day, presenting myself to her in a kind of working shirt and pants in a lion yellow colour. When our friend spontaneously told B this, she understood the signal. During the final years of my physical life, I had a pair of lion yellow trousers that I used to like very much as they were pleasant to wear. The working shirt reminded B of how I had worn a shirt like this when I was involved in the move to our new home. Now she understood that I wished to help her through a hard passage and that this too was a crucial moment.

Now B was able to receive the flow of energy and was calibrating with me as soul. Like me she found that the noise around her was unimportant and no more than a distraction. Late that evening, she opened herself to how the now familiar crystal energy came in through the crown chakra as a high frequency, incorruptible and penetrating energy, feeling like a sharp point. I felt what she felt and knew that this was different compared to our meeting that morning. It was of a different quality. What happened now went beyond our own soul relationship.

The spiritual world was addressing B but I was with her when it happened. We were invited to some kind of council. Many light beings were there, and B was both able to see and hear. She was told that she was to transfuse these high, tingling energies. We were both honoured to take part. After some time, we were shown a kind of portal. On the other side of the portal were other worlds where we could exist together. The words came to B:

– *If I am worthy – open the door!*

She repeated this three times. Open for her to see was how she and I met as man and woman in energy. It was like a continuation of our soul meeting in the morning, but now totally in these higher energies. Everything was energy. On behalf of us both, B expressed gratitude for the blessing given to us and our shared purpose.

The transmission from the spiritual world continued. Master Kuthumi approached as he had done since many years to B. His sign is an intense light beam coming in to the crown chakra slightly from the right. In the midst of his love, he often expresses himself as determined and powerful with no fuss. This time he only said:

— This (the book) is to be published!

These words and all that had gone before started a creative flow and the structure of the book began to show. Like everything, it was already there on the energy level. Now it was to be manifested through B and it was crucial that she was in high enough energies to be able to accomplish this. The separate chapters flowed one after the other. It was like a cork had left the bottle. After this, B understood that she had passed the test and been raised in energy. All the distractions along the path had been a portal she was supposed to go through. She realised that some of her foolish priorities in daily life had to do with fear.

The day after, the flow came through and I was now able to transmit my words concerning the book and our writing together.

— This book will be written from within. There is no other way. It is good that you, like you are doing now, connect with me and that we exchange energies as a start of your writing. It is likely to be like that every time. When you approach it from a more conventional place of ambition then the flow will stop.

To write is meant to be joyous!

These words inspired B to tell about us and quality of enjoyment. This moment together was the first that she wrote about and it became the prologue of our book *Love Beyond Death*. The flow continued.

A few days later, Master Kuthumi approached us again and transmitted:

— You as a couple are important. Couples like you are needed in these times. Many have the opportunity. Inspire them!

Our united heart merged with the universal heart where the love of Master Kuthumi poured in. We received love and blessings for our life task.

All landmarks

are now

left behind

Life on Earth is most often defined via our three lowest chakras of physical survival, sexuality and power. 'Lower' does not mean that these chakras are less important. They constitutes a vitality and a force that the other chakras need. However, these three chakras need to be governed by higher energies so their forces will develop in the beautiful way they are meant to. Many spiritual traditions tell that the actual meaning of the spiritual journey is living and working on Earth but not 'being of it'. By that, I mean to let the higher energies govern life on Earth. In practice, this demands a high degree of focus and being prepared to leave old ways of relating to life. Parallel to the now flowing writing of our book *Love Beyond Death*, another process was intensified, about letting go of the last remains of identification with the physical body and the physical life on Earth.

To let go of old thought patterns

When B and I were living on Earth together, we shared many moments of pleasure – this was an important part of our relationship. Together we'd enjoyed what nature had to offer, spending time together and delicious meals. Before we met as Man & Woman, we had each experienced loneliness in the midst of other people. That feeling disappeared totally during our more than thirty years together as a couple, and it did not even show up in times of disagreement. In the home we shared, we used to sit in each our sofa communicating for hours in a way that gave us both a sense of meaning. For B, these moments had been the hardest to release.

It was now three years after my passing and we had reached far in the development of our soul marriage. Still, in some situations old thought patterns were there. As a way to let go of these old patterns, B travelled to San Francisco and to Esalen. This place is in many ways the cradle of what is called the *Human Potential Movement* of which Gestalt therapy plays a part. This journey was about closing circles concerning the most valuable parts of our life together, such as moments of pleasure and the visiting of places that were linked to our working life.

In a restaurant at the harbour of San Francisco, where B was enjoying a delicious lobster soup, I approached her and transmitted:

– One reason why you are going on this journey is to let go of thoughts of loneliness. Actually, you are not alone. We are together always and I enjoy being with you.

Through B consciously placing herself in environments that we as an Earthly couple had most enjoyed, we were able to unite these earthly memories with the fellowship as souls that we now shared. B soon realised that we were there together in energy. On the surface, she was sitting there alone, but in energy we were both enjoying the view, the lobster and the taste of white wine. As soul, there are no limits regarding where we can meet. On the contrary, freedom and exchange during travels grow as they take you away from old habits that otherwise would stop the exchange. Our shared spiritual journey is extremely physical. This is our path, and to B it is essential. What you experience in your body is not possible to deny as if it were fantasy. The body cannot lie.

Our days in San Francisco continued with valuable experiences, both of the city and of each other. Still, what happened at the airport on the way to Monterey was the most surprising. In the midst of a crowd of people, our soul meeting from the morning continued. During our stay in San Francisco, B again and again had experienced how unconditional love was crumbling all old thought patterns, patterns linked to worries and loneliness. This love was also expressed in the way strangers took care of her in this environment that was filled with lovely memories and nostalgia. At the airport, it was not me but other light beings that approached B while she was sitting on a bench in the departure hall. They transmitted to her:

— *You don´t see your own greatness, and paradoxically this is your greatness. Heart and love are your focus. Your body is becoming more and more light. This means that you are becoming more and more useful to us, and this is especially valuable because of the soul union between you and your husband, this union you hold within your physical body. You are uniting Heaven & Earth and Man & Woman. This means that wherever you go, we are able to work through you as a kind of transformer or GPS. You don´t have to understand through your intellect. It is enough that you physically are there.*

What you and your husband have merged is unusual and we hope more couples will be similarly inspired. As time passes, you will travel to places and be in situations where people will understand. Your book is a part of this. Maybe you will start by being in such a place for a month, perhaps longer.

Simultaneously, waves of energy flowed through her physical body while she was surrounded by people at the airport. B asked who was speaking and received this answer:

— *We are several. Your husband, of course, is always with you. Master Kuthumi, Master Sananda and me, Mary.*

B felt that it was a woman but was to begin with unsure about which Mary it was, Mother Mary or Mary Magdalen, although she reminded herself that she had brought a book about Mary Magdalene. Still she felt support in her situation from both light beings, Mother Mary and

Mary Magdalene. It was especially valuable as she was filled with wonder and joy and she also felt there was much to relate to and to embrace. As reinforcement, more words followed:

— *We will inspire you to travel to different places where you need to be so we will be able to work through you.*

The transmission continued until late that evening when we arrived at the beautiful beach of Monterey. This teaching was from woman to woman.

The time we spent at Esalen became like balm for the soul to both of us. This beautiful and dear place on the western coast of California south of San Francisco gave us the opportunity to relive much of the joy and meaning that had been at the foundation of our life together. The transformation and transition into our new soul life had come about in a variety of ways. We had experienced how a new generation was now doing what we used to, so we could let go; experiencing their wonderful energy helped. And B got help for her physical body – body treatments and a bath in hot springs – important for letting go of old patterns and helping B to find freedom in dancing wildly for the first time in many years.

The light beings that had approached B at the airport had shown how we were supposed to contribute in our new life. Old thought patterns from before (that we ourselves physically were going out in the world to contribute) no longer applied. Instead, the focus was on being as clean an instrument as possible and letting the spiritual world work through the physical body and through our soul union.

On the way home, we again stopped at the beach in Monterey. Filled with the strong experiences from the time at Esalen, B was open when an invitation to an inner ceremony was offered. We celebrated that we now had arrived at our new life and had released what had been of meaning to us in our old life. A new state of consciousness developed that revived an old memory from an earlier life when B was a priestess in Egypt. I have told about that earlier life in the chapter about our journey to Egypt.

The ceremony we were now remembering through cell memories in the physical body related to the priestess having a love meeting with the cosmos itself via her navel. We were both part of this ceremony; B as a woman and I as a man. The process was distinct, as if we were being taught at the same time. Finally, B surrendered her rose to me as a man, the greatest thing a man can ever experience. A couple of years later, this surrender would be shown to be vital to the further union of our souls' energies.

The energy from our ceremony continued to flow in the physical body. When we arrived home from our journey, we were living our new life and old patterns were gone. Instead, these intense energies were alive in the body. Old cell memories that had been awakened created security and joy in the present life.

All landmarks are now left

Easter came shortly after our journey to Esalen. This was an opportunity to further deepen our soul relationship by going to a retreat. There, with others, we lived in crystal energy in meditation, in the dimension where we remembered being the same energy body. Through the Masters and other Light beings, we were told how important it is in this time to live in trust and not become fragmented. During one meditation, B met me from another incarnation. We were there in our light bodies and also with other friends. Again, we were blessed in our life task. These light beings spoke to B:

— You came here with both of you. And he was already here with you both. You are a hologram of each other. It will all the more be like that for everyone. You are just living this in a very concrete way.

During the next meditation, we birthed ourselves together into a new dimension. The same morning B had experienced how the area above the ears of the physical body was changed. Simultaneously, her head was filled with extremely high energies and her ears with a tingling sound. During the meditation, her hands encircled the stomach and uterus and there was a feeling that the umbilical cord was linked to the galaxy. As an embryo, we were raised to a higher sphere and were born into that dimension. In this frequency we had completely left Earth's gravity and were able to fly together.

When we had left the retreat and arrived back home in the physical world, I transmitted to B:

— Dear little dove! Now you are able to fly and I am happy that we can experience ourselves as Man & Woman and still exist in another world than the one you live in. We have received an initiation to a higher level, but that does not stop us from enjoying each other. It started with the conception that was birthing us into a new sphere. Now in peace, we will be able to manifest. I am your man and lover forever.

Our union was living intensely in the midst of daily life. Old moments of worries were gone. Since a few months it had become possible for B to leave the main office of the consultancy company. Even the little office that after the move became a temporary place would be left and B was now looking forward to renting a room of her own in an office in the city centre. It was now time to create an environment in alignment with our new life. We met in our light bodies day and night knowing that we were together on Earth as well as where I exist as soul with no physical body. One evening, after one of these intense moments, we both heard these words from far away:

– *All landmarks are now left!*

To B the words came from such a distance that she was at first not able to give them meaning. She needed to bring the words to her brain to be able to understand what was said. Before that moment, I had specifically asked her to wait. There was something important I wished to show her. It was as if I raised her up in energy to make her feel that we are one and the same. Then I let our union come back to her physical body and all the energy points linking us to it. That was the moment when the words came to her and me simultaneously.

The next morning, the same words again came to B. She confirmed the words and surrendered to me. She felt as if she had been lifted from the ground and was flying. A new moment arose between us, in total stillness, and I transmitted to her:

– *This moment is to be treasured as it is. It is profound. Let us together bless what has happened to us.*

That morning, it took some time before B was able to look out into the world around her. There was a kind of milky mist in the room and our shared light bubble withheld us from the outer world, although we were still aware of it. Later, when B sat down to write, her hand shook from the energies. She was happy and visualised how our book was to be published the coming year. Then all situations that included outer considerations were to be left and our new life would begin.

124

The living emptiness

In step with the fact that outer obstacles had disappeared, B more and more came to the state of consciousness where I am now living. In this consciousness, beyond time and space, I exist in a living emptiness. This is an emptiness for creation of anything that is to manifest. This was a strong experience for B and it affected her daily life to a high degree. It turned into a creation and a choice in every second. There is an enormous potential in this and simultaneously a great responsibility.

Living on Earth and at the same time existing in living emptiness is quite demanding. A few people we know live in a similar way. To B, the feeling often came of being a guest in a reality that is no longer her real one. At the same time, we enjoyed our togetherness in energy. It provided our foundation for living. The task became to weave light threads between the worlds.

B's physical body became more sensitive and reacted with a deep cough. As more and more light flowed into its cells, old stuff needed to get out. There was now a safe stability in that we as souls were always together. B was able to stop looking for confirmation from books and others who had maybe experienced something similar. For some time, Master Kuthumi had asked her to trust her own experience – he could be quite harsh in this. Writing our book strengthened her understanding of how much we had been through. At the same time as writing, B was still working as a consultant and a therapist as well as phasing out her consultancy company. She gave the physical body the necessary attention so the energy flows could come through.

One morning I approached her to remind her of where we were now in our shared soul journey:

– *I have been with you during the whole night as you can feel. We meet like this now, so nothing will disturb the*

125

light flowing into your cells. There is nothing wrong with our passionate soul meetings, they are only of different frequencies. You are going through a lot now. The light will penetrate everything. You are arranging it well for us. Don´t worry about that book you are reading – the writers of such books are following their path, we ours. Focus on the light that will fill this whole body. The rest follows from that. My little dove – I love you! We are one now and forever. But you know this now and feel safe.

Through the light, our soul union was now going deeper into the physical body. Also, my part of our union started to express itself in the physical body, felt as special memories or sensitivities. What we did not know at that time was how this would develop even more later.

Our soul union seen from outside by our clairvoyant friends

One of our clairvoyant friends (who had been with us since many years) had made an appointment with B at her new office. It was meant as a meeting between two old friends, but from habit it turned into a consultation so B was able to partake in how our friend now experienced me and B in spirit. This time B was confident in herself, but she still enjoyed this meeting between the three of us as it developed, as I in these sessions speak through and show myself to our friend.

Our friend saw me stand behind B and saw me kissing her on her cheek, quite physical and close. I usually present myself to our friend in different shirts at different times and did so also that day. There is a special kind of humour between us doing this. I told her how B and I now flow together. Our friend used the word 'synthesis' to describe this to B. This is what I describe as us being one and the same heart. Our friend saw that

126

now obstacles were gone, both inner and outer, and that I had been with B in all this. She also pointed out that this is unusual and that we have a very strong relationship. I showed her how it was when we had just met, and that I as a physical man at that time did not have the courage to express myself as clearly as I do now, especially regarding how much I loved B and how lovely I felt she was.

I showed my friend how I exist now as soul. I have let go of layer by layer and I am young in body and mind. I showed her a beautiful green landscape and oceans. She understood that I am fulfilled and happy where I am and that I am now living in the freedom that I longed for in my physical life. Now I realise that I at that time kept a memory of how it is here and that I did not want to adjust to the demands of Earth.

He is putting words into your mouth! Through me our friend could see how that had happened and B recognised the same from our soul meetings. Our friend saw the big changes that had happened within B during the latest year and how important our shared life task is. When it came to writing, in her inner mind she saw three small books in white and gold. To her, it meant that they already existed in energy. She saw how B collected her material from different diaries, highlighting certain parts, and that those parts created the text to come. B's soul brother L also presented himself to our friend. He showed that he continued to hold the energy for us and our life task.

Our friend saw three books in a line. What we did not know at that time was that the first of these was already complete and that this book would clear the path for the other two. At that time, we thought that the first one would be more extensive and that the other two would contain a deepening of different themes. Her reading was of great help to us in this as the great challenges during the coming summer made writing totally impossible.

Make visible — no revenge!

Most people on Earth long for peace. The horror of war and its meaninglessness is obvious to almost everyone. In our time, as well as throughout the history of man, there are forces that seek to work for a more humane world. At the same time, there are also destructive forces that tear down and destroy. These destructive forces exist in all of us. They are built on fear and survival, experienced as the law of the jungle.

In olden times, people believed in the old adage 'an eye for an eye and a tooth for a tooth'. This resulted in bloody family fights that turned into bigger wars. When we seek revenge, we become as hateful as those we wish to punish. It turns into an endless spiral of evil in which both parties consider they have the right to punish and kill. Humanity today claims to have progressed further and wishes to create peace through diplomacy and dialogue. In this way, many wars have been avoided even if the intention not always has been as peaceful as it appears on the surface. Greediness and power are to a high degree behind these cold wars. It gets in the way to agree in a true way.

Fundamentalism in politics or religion makes it especially hard to create a shared future. Fundamentalism includes the conviction that you are always right and the other person is always wrong. This point of view makes it necessary to shelter your own sphere of interest from anticipated attack, and this way of relating to life exists among different countries, peoples and religions. It also exists between individuals functioning in this way. In today's world, the biggest gap is not primarily between religions and countries but between individuals and groups relating in a fundamentalist way in contrast to people who are prepared to create solutions together. That is why great efforts to create peace seem at first to function and later collapse when the peacemakers try to anchor agreements in their respective populations.

These different views and ways of relating to life meet on an individual level, group level and within organisations. As humans we behave in the same way in a diplomatic context, within governments, work life and private life. It boils down to the will and ability to live and view life from the other person's perspective. This is necessary for dialogue and without this, dialogue dies. A lack of perspective has its root in being closed off from our own feelings due to fear, and in turn that fear has also been closed off. The mechanism is understandable, but what happens to the people concerned?

When we were both living on Earth, B and I worked a lot to create dialogue between people in their private lives, as well as in their professional environments. We were inspired by Gestalt philosophy and a methodology based on dialectics, existentialism and phenomenology. We had a faith (almost a magic faith) that this in the long run would create peace. As long as we worked with people who, to some degree, were able to live from the viewpoint of the other, we experienced great progress. But we also were confronted with situations that came into an abrupt stop. We learnt that some people aren't able to see beyond their own point of view and they view their own experience as the truth for everyone. When this happened, powerlessness filled the room, both within us and within those who in one way or another were dependent on these persons. Each individual has their own responsibility (at least when it comes to adults) to decide how they wish to live their life. Working with couples, this might mean the end of the relationship when it became clear that only one point of view was possible and that the truth of the other did not exist in the eyes of their partner.

Make visible – no revenge

During her private and working life, B had experiences that made it necessary to leave situations for the reasons I mentioned above. These were hard decisions as we had such a strong faith in dialogue as a tool and that personal encounters would usually help. Through inner spiritual guidance, B received a way to relate in those situations that had rendered her powerless. We receive these challenges as portals for our growth. That is why it is so important to find ways to meet them so we are raised in energy instead of getting into personal conflict.

Many years ago, a colleague, for a variety of reasons, had secretly intended to take over the business B worked in. When these plans surfaced, it created a fear that such totally different values would destroy decades of non-profit work. Unexpectedly, inner guidance appeared early one morning in a taxi. B was then shown how she and her colleague were fencing, dressed in clothes from another era. In the midst of this, a voice approached her and transmitted:

– You are now able to choose between fighting and being the one who sits in the gallery and watches. Try here and now to go back and forth between these positions! Your task is to make visible – no revenge!

These words were of great help to the situation and continued to stay with her into future occasions when she felt powerless. Once the situation was clear to them, they were more inclined to accept responsibility. The fullness of time would show the final results. In fact, the results were not the most important thing but how B related to the situation. That is how our soul grows.

Later, similar situations occurred. The wisdom of 'make visible – no revenge' has been of great value. This does not imply that it has been easy. It has been essential to

132

ask for help from the spiritual world, to ask for a loving resolution and let go of our own ideas how to achieve that. During our lives on Earth, we all face situations that we're not able to resolve on a personal level. We need the perspective and the energies from the spiritual world for those tangled knots to be untied. In our despair, we as humans can surrender to higher forces and let them resolve any situation created on the personal plane. At the same time, we have to let go of our need to control outcomes and instead mourn that it was not possible to reach each other on a personal level.

The book *Love Beyond Death* is birthed

B was to encounter her own fears of publishing our book. These fears came both from her present life on Earth and from other lives when it was dangerous to recount experiences and thoughts of the kind that this book describes. An old fear brought anxiety into her present life. However, there also was reason behind this anxiety. In a society based on a scientific world view, many talk in a contemptuous way about phenomena that are beyond the accepted. In our secular Scandinavian society, we have been taught to be neutral towards religions and religious views of life. However, the same freedom is not there when you (as in our book) describe your own experiences. Maybe it comes too close to the bone?

We had come close in merging our souls´ energies, and I wished to show B how this might express itself. I knew that this would give her security and help her through her portal of fears.

She was driving the car to our summer cottage when I approached her in energy. I played a little with her by influencing her way of driving at the same time as I came close to her. Her reaction came immediately. She felt a flow and a more firm way of driving than her own, and she felt my presence. When we both lived on Earth, I hardly let go of the steering wheel – it was an ongoing joke between us. As soul, I (of course) didn't take over the steering wheel, but my energy affected B and she noticed the difference.

Then I sent a picture to B so she would understand in what way I could be close to her. I showed how I existed in a kind of soap bubble with a thin veil. This thin veil is the boundary between our parallel worlds. It is necessary so B would not disappear to where I am. In my bubble there is no time and space. I am able to be part of life on Earth when people are in the now, beyond time and space. From where I am, I see all this while I am invisible to most people, although not to all. This time, B had the opportunity to also see, while usually she only senses and hears. It became even clearer to her how close we were. Her physical heart was widening in a powerful way creating a deep cough. We continued to float, driving along. Later, we arrived together at the summer cottage.

For B, that summer included facing a new situation of powerlessness that to her was emotionally difficult. This time she did not even have time to ask the spiritual world for help. We were there directly with her and raised her by sending such high energies to her that she was not able to speak a word during the meeting. It was meant to be this way. During the following night and day, she lived with us in a compact energy bubble and her physical body reacted. It felt like fire in her head and in the area above her ears.

Later, when B was sitting on a bench at the summer cottage gazing over the sea that was bright as a mirror, I approached her and linked the energies in the head with her whole spine and back. I transmitted to her:

— You are no longer allowed to engage in personal conflict. That is why you were blocked during our conversation and we raised you to another level of frequency. You cannot and should not try to resolve this on a personal level. You are a vessel for what is happening and it influences more than the two of you. You were supposed to be totally emptied of the personal level of this issue. That is why it happened like this.

B's physical body reacted heavily within and above her heart, which was widened and it hurt. Sadness and love lived there together. B understood that she had been through a challenge that concerned unconditional love.

The summer continued and B was grateful that she had been carried through the pain behind her powerlessness. She understood that only the energies of Heaven are able to deal with this situation. She had been raised up and was filled with intense energies, especially in her head. On one occasion, she was on the veranda of our summer cottage where we as a physical couple had experienced many loving moments. The memory came to her; I was close and I spoke to her:

— We meet like this now. I am within you and we are melting together.

Her physical body was filled with our energies throughout the whole light pillar and lower back. While these waves were going through her body, the energy became stronger in her heart and thymus as the meeting point for our exchange. I continued my transmission:

— We create in love and light. I am within you and with you in everything you do!

Baptism by fire

It was time for a retreat on our way home from the summer cottage. Our friend from Holland was coming with her meditation group and we were welcomed to join. B was wakened very early that morning by a new kind of intense energy that came into her head and lit up there. It was so powerful that she could hardly bear it. She noticed that her stomach had started to react and tried to focus in her heart to be able to receive there. She stayed for a while in bed but the reaction came anyway.

The energy beam was evidently the start of the retreat. B's physical body reacted with vomiting and diarrhoea and total exhaustion. Fortunately, our friend could drive the car to the retreat. Apparently, this was a cleansing after what had happened during the summer and to prepare for the coming days. After arrival, there was nothing she could do but go to bed while the others started their first meditation. B was well taken care of by the leader of the retreat, an old friend of ours. She received a medicine from the Amazon jungle and our clairvoyant friend described what she perceived:

– You have what I call the 'fever of the soul'. Your light body has reacted with inflammation due to deep sadness.

The morning after, B's body had recovered and we were able to join the group. This day started with the invitation to receive directly from solar energy. It was a continuation of the earlier meditations where we'd received crystal energy directly into the water of the physical body. Receiving directly from solar energy was powerful. The message of the meditation was clear: the greatest responsibility of every soul is to keep its own frequency and not allow itself to be pulled down. Every soul has its own path to follow and we as souls are not allowed to make judgements of the paths of others.

These words were directed to all humanity. The message emphasised discernment and the necessity to use our spiritual sword. Our greatest responsibility is to be God in our own Universe, to develop the ability to love all our cells and to let in the divine love that is always there for us.

I approached B during the meditation and we floated together in a waving dance. The dance was about the joy that she had now let go of her heaviness. I spoke seriously to her and transmitted that she was no longer allowed to make herself heavy like she just had done. It affects us both as instrument as we are united and react together. It would stop our contribution to the divine plan. She was happy to meet me like this and grateful that she had been carried through it all.

At the end of the meditation, more light beings came, Masters and angels. Master Sananda spoke to B:

– *Your task is to live in the love that you now are receiving and let yourself be filled and enjoy. Show on Earth how it is to receive divine love. Show them with who you are!*

After this transmission the fears of publishing our book disappeared. The issue became unimportant in relation to this great gift, to receive and bring further divine love. In the same way, the whole group was lifted as a team about to go out in the world with this enormous protection of divine love. Driving back to our little home was like floating. It was as if we were carried all the way.

Summer was long that year and we enjoyed swimming in the sea close to home. It was wonderful to be together in our own little temple. Our soul love meetings were natural, calm and filled with great tenderness. We were already together so they acted as a lovely reminder. Often, I let B listen to melodies on the radio that made her feel my presence, and found her some male tenors singing love songs – such singers are a link between us.

One evening on the balcony, B was sitting and reflecting on what had happened. I gave her the impulse to remember *timelines* that had been apparent when we were manifesting our new home. Now it was about seeing the timeline of what had happened and being prepared to use her *spiritual sword*, keeping the boundaries but not taking revenge. Her physical body reacted powerfully to this transmission. It was as if Heaven and Earth had met in her body, and she felt as if her body was on fire and that all was dissolved in love. Her heart widened even more. In this way, B's physical body received healing energies and she fell into a peaceful sleep, covered in a warm blanket. The next day, B was busy writing our book. She thanked me that I had carried her through her hard time and I spoke to her:

– *Where I am we don´t feel anxiety as you do on Earth. But we are dependent on each other and it is imperative that you let go. From your love you offered a second opportunity. What will come from that is beyond your influence. 'The baptism of fire' was necessary and we go through it together.*

You have a good structure for your writing and you are in flow. You also have developed yourself further so you are moving much more freely. I enjoy being with you. I love you, little dove!

We enjoy our time here in our little home. It is meant for us to be here in stillness, you and I. You have been our outpost all summer when we met with other people. That is fine and now is our time. The balcony has become a harmonic place for us, our place. Here you are not allowed to be disturbed. So keep your boundaries. You will.

Cleansing by swimming in the sea

The unusual warm late summer offered wonderful opportunities for ceremonial cleansing baths that became a natural part of the process after the baptism of fire that had entailed cutting threads from the old life. At the same time, it meant welcoming the energy body that had long ago become visible for us during meditation. In this energy body, we were one and the same, and now we welcomed it into the physical body. Through that, freedom and lightness arose.

Swimming in the morning had meant an inner process to B in which she had stopped identifying with her old life and instead welcomed our united energy body as her inner identity. That same afternoon, again on her way to bathe, she stopped in front of the photo of me as Mikael and felt an overwhelming love. At the same time it became obvious how long had passed since we'd met physically and how strong our soul relationship now was. She welcomed that our shared energy body now has its home also in the physical body. That day's second cleansing bath was about my role in what happened.

The writing of our book continued. As so often, the parallels became visible between what was written about and what was happening in the now while writing. We saw that there was meaning behind this and that our understanding deepens through the writing. Much of what was told to B many years ago was now happening. A totally new life was to bloom in the year 2016 – there was one more year to go. The cleansing baths were an important part of the transformation.

The following day, we met again in soul energy. It was drizzling outside so we stayed indoors listening to melodies that I summoned. Then B put down her paper and leaned back on her chair. Her hands were moving as if they were talking to each other; they were in a variety of ways linking us to the energy body we share.

I spoke to B:

— You are holding the energy for our shared energy body that is us in that frequency. It has now moved into the physical body. It does not mean that we will stop making love to each other on a soul level, but it will be different. You will be a pure receiver as woman. I as man in soul will give to you and help you to keep your body young and sensual. Enjoy and receive me as the man I am in soul, but with this change in our being together. Notice how I approach you now beginning with the navel.

We have travelled far, my love! Your navel is now strongly linked to Universe and is vibrating in that energy. Also, feel how my male soul energy fills your ovaries and uterus with light.

You will now become a pure receiver in a vibrating body and we will continue to create in energy and light. It will take time before people will understand you on Earth. This is why we will be close in this way to each other and live our lives together.

The only initiative that came from B during this transmission and love soul meeting was to give her rose to me and to Universe. Once more B was filled with wonder of a process that was far beyond what the intellect could ever create. 'Miracle' was the word that spontaneously came from B, and she placed our shared experience far away to the third book. Joy and the energy from our soul meetings now became the foundation for her daily life.

In the midst of B's writing, I approached her again and transmitted:

— Don´t forget that you are a goddess! You find it difficult to realise that and be open about it. But this is not boasting. Everyone has a god, a divine part within. Most people

140

don't make contact with it. Whenever I approach you I come to you as a god, as a divine force. That is why we are able to create together, because we meet in our divinity and unite that with the earthly so all will be one.

Do you notice that you vibrate in the forehead and directly down to the navel? This is only possible when you live in your divinity. Orgasm is possible all over the body, even in the forehead, head and crown.

B understood that I was more active than ever for her physical body to be kept alive and receptive to these high energies. She felt that a shakeup was going on that related to her physical body. I also gave her the impulse to read a text that helped her feel the great meaning of writing our book:

– God is love, we receive that love. We see glimpses of it here on Earth. What love requires of us is to tell that nobody is alone.

When these words had reached the bottom of the heart, it became natural to B to write that it was the only answer to the great gift that she and I have. *Love requires to tell…* She realised that she was not allowed to forget who she was as soul, that she was here to tell that death is not what most people believe, that we understand this when we dare to embrace, that we all carry a divine spark within that is possible to make contact with and be led by. All is there if we dare to open ourselves to it.

The next morning B woke up in the midst of a transmission of high energies into her physical body. She understood that she once more had been receiving energies during the night. When she opened herself even more to the energies and let them come in, a picture of me as Mikael and as a little boy appeared. B met me in the vulnerable part of the man I had been when we were a physical couple. Love to the little boy that I once was poured from B and was strengthened by the love from our shared energy body that folded its wings around him. That part that once was me was now loved and held forever. It was a release that filled us both and it happened through the union of personal love from B with universal love from us both.

Inner

ceremonies with

our Masters

It was now time for a new and totally crucial step of our souls' journey to the highest light.

What happened was beyond our imagination, even for me who already was in the light. We develop as souls after our passing, but it happens in a slightly different way compared to when you live on Earth in a physical body. Taking this new step together, we needed help in a more direct way, focusing on our specific task as part of the greater divine plan. It is told that the Master will appear when the apprentice is ripe and so it happened. Now a spiritual guide crossed our path, a woman who had the gift to see us in our entirety and what the path of our souls was about. She was naturally connected to the Masters who had long been with us. Their cooperation between Heaven & Earth, including our souls, became like a spiritual embrace. Now we were safe to continue.

Receiving this powerful assistance in such a concrete way was a great liberation and created the needed calm for us to live through what was happening. It was like going to therapy from a soul level and for the growth of the soul, both as individual souls and as a kind of couple therapy. At the same time, we were offered our own place where our joy could flower, the joy of all we have received and experienced. This was a luxury to us who otherwise kept this joy to ourselves.

Our commitment is to, through our souls' energies, unite Heaven & Earth and Man & Woman – letting all polarities melt into the One. When writing *Union of Souls* B and I have reached this midpoint of polarities on our souls' journey. This is a state of consciousness and a perspective that is a prerequisite for writing this book. We arrived at this point during a journey to India where we'd reached the culmination of a twelve year long inner journey. Since then, our flow has been calibrated and is now calm and stable. Every closure is a new beginning. What this means will be shown later. Now on our path

146

to the point between all polarities, we received help to calibrate the energies.

When the energies of the soul are about to merge with the physical energies of the body, it is not an abstract event but something concrete and tangible. The energies of the soul influence the body and vice versa. For many years, B had surrendered her physical body as a vessel and an instrument for our shared task. Many people on Earth live in the same way. They live on Earth but are identified in their soul and not in their physical body. To us it was about calibrating both our souls with the physical body still on Earth. We understood from what had already happened that the higher B and her physical body were raised in energy, the closer to Earth my soul energy could come. Now the situation was acute.

You need to remember that the energies of the soul follow different laws to physical earthly ones. Soul energy can exist everywhere in the same moment. It brings with it everything that it has ever been united with, and all exists simultaneously. The higher the frequency of soul energy moves, the lighter and freer the experience. Heavier energies from fears expressed as worries, doubts and criticism cannot remain. The healing of these wounds is a part of the journey of the soul. They transform into wisdom and love and join the soul. In the highest light, where the divine part of the souls exist, there is endless space. This means that the innermost essence of the soul is kept at the same time as it is calibrated with other souls in that frequency. In the end, this goes for all souls. When we as humanity meet there, we will remember who we are and that we are all a hologram to each other. B's and my task and our souls' journey is an example of this being experienced in a concrete way.

Ceremonies with our Masters

When visiting our spiritual guide, the Masters who had been close to us on our path approached us in a tangible way. Master Kuthumi was guiding us as well as Master St Germain (who is close to our spiritual guide). All three of us have had the privilege to meet Master Sananda during great times of transformation in our lives.

Master Kuthumi stated that we as souls at first need to merge with the highest light before it is possible to calibrate with the physical body. Otherwise, the physical body would experience pain and hurt. All the years of stiffness in the physical body was related to this process. To be able to merge with the highest light, B needed to let go of everything on Earth that made her heavy and caught up in physical life, including the little things of daily life. Master Kuthumi guided us in concrete ways and told us to create three to five occasions of intimate meditation. In meditation, we were guided to walk towards the highest light and stand still at a portal with a table in front. Someone would meet us there. Master Kuthumi described in words the longing I felt as M to be able to merge with B in this way. This was a solemn occasion for us both. Together we received wisdom from the Masters and felt great support on our path.

The same evening we met in intimate meditation and we were walking towards the highest light. Master Kuthumi and Master St Germain were present holding the space and energy for us. B saw the portal and the table like an altar. She knew that Master Sananda would come, but this was not to happen on this occasion. There was a personal issue B had to let go of. She put her hands together in prayer and surrendered the situation to Master Sananda and the energies of the spiritual world. Her unconditional love was included in her surrender.

After a long night, totally in our own world and far from all imaginable disturbances, we again met in meditation and returned to the same place. B expressed her longing to melt together with my soul energy, saying that she was prepared to let this union come into the physical body and that it would be a joint decision when to ascend and go back to the home of our souls. I was very close and spoke to her:

— Our session yesterday with our spiritual guide was extremely important. Now we both understand what is happening and are able to live from there and choose. I am longing to merge with you and I am waiting for you. It is harder on Earth, I understand that. I love you forever!

Then the unbelievable happened! The hands were lifted to the sky, palms facing. Then they came together and we merged in energy. Simultaneously, we both saw the portal from above with an altar in front. Master Sananda was there and he held the ceremony for our soul wedding as the bride and groom we were there. We were standing in a strong white light. The hands accompanied the event by crossing and caressing both cheeks and it was not possible to know which hand was on which cheek. The energies were flowing over the physical body and we were creating in light and love. B expressed that from this moment both our impulses would count equally in the physical body.

Nothing was like before after what we had been through – we both felt the same. My soul energy now had come closer to the Earth and B felt all the more what I felt and I what she felt. The experience of us both as alive in the same physical body was mind-blowing. We both knew that it was all about soul energies, but the link to the physical body created an experience that became almost physical. We both understood that we would encounter a period of time focused on calibration between us. Living this calibration, we would each feel the other's feelings. I transmitted to B:

– *You can do what you need to do in the outer world, but it is important that you follow both the rhythm of my being in the light and your own rhythm when we are in alignment. When you make a break and become still, we will meet in the light more clearly and this will also give you nourishment so you will be able to face the outer world. You have been on your way to let go of being governed from the outer world. Now it is like that all the way. It is about how we will meet the outer world.*

As Master Kuthumi had predicted, we met in meditation three more times at the same inner place. We then experienced the event from different perspectives. The first time we saw us as bride and groom in soul from above, the second time we experienced how I as the groom came from the left and merged with the bride, and the third time we saw ourselves being merged from behind. After that we experienced it all in the physical body.

Since my passing, my presence as soul had been on B's left side while I had been influencing her right side to surrender to the divine plan. What happened during these inner ceremonies was that our soul energies merged and my male soul energy found its place, mainly on the right side of the physical body.

The calibration between our soul energies continued during the months after the ceremonies that we had experienced together. Daily, we received light to the physical body, and in step with that we were raised together. These delicate energies poured into the throat, the navel and back and were widening these areas. On

150

one such occasion, I transmitted to B:

— Now rest your right arm and shoulder. I embrace your shoulder in the same way as I used to while we met on Earth, only from in front now. It is time for me to take over and lead us so your right shoulder gets to rest as it has been working too hard. We are now united in soul and my energy is here.

It will be easier for you now, less painful. You are a courageous woman! Not many would do what you do. It demands a lot from you. And we have chosen this path. It is the greatest a man and a woman can experience together. This is a culmination of many incarnations, when we in a few of them have been together as king and queen. Our grandchild is right – we are both used to ruling. In our most recent life I did not wish to lead. You did that a lot and you need to let go now. From here I am happy to lead us both. It's so different in these frequencies; it is not like governing on Earth. We flow together and work together.

We merge with the physical body during a long and still moment like this. This is a solemn occasion. Our soul energies merge with all the cells in the physical body.

Day and night, the physical body was filled with light. It was evident that it was about receiving without understanding what it was about. Our inner life together existed most of day and night while the outer life was going on in full force. One way or another it became possible. As soon as there was a calm moment, we met in intense light bubbles that filled the physical body and made it light and soft while our souls vibrated from love and joy.

On a later occasion, when the daily filling of light had been going on for a couple of months, we expressed our gratitude to our Masters, who had been with us, and we met in the wonder of how we were able to experience our soul energies through the physical body. For some time, we had experienced our united heart. Now this union had spread to other parts of the physical body. This body was beginning to feel androgynous as it was now a place for both our souls to find expression. This was beyond what either of us could ever imagine, even I was now in totally new territory. At the end we both experienced how the physical body was stretched out, as if it were lying on a bed. This moment transferred into an initiation by Master Sananda who touched the forehead and transmitted:

– This is the sign! The light is healing all the darkness!

He said these words three times and simultaneously we were shown the wings of Isis. We understood that we had been filled by the highest light and we now were able to heal through that light. The following night there was an addition to the wings of Isis. It was a triangle with a heart placed upside down. When this was shown, again came the words that this was the sign. We continued to receive from this enormous light. The more we received, the more we got flashes from earlier lives together when we had been living in this light. We merged with these lives and got power and inspiration to our life now.

Our soul union
in the midst of tasks in the outer world

B was surprised that we were supposed to take on two big commitments in the midst of an extremely intense period of inner soul work. From my perspective, it would fill several important functions. I wished to show her that we were able to live with our inner process in the midst of an intense outer world. As long as we are consciously together

152

in energy and come from our own platform, everything is possible. Then we live and work from the energies of heart and light. What had been disruptive from time to time was when B had let herself be influenced by inner and outer forces based on fear. Now we were so close to each other in our soul energies, it was easy for me to react and lead us to our united energy.

The calibration of soul energies with the physical body was a radical experience for both of us. To B, who was the one who was visible to most people, it concerned, in a concrete way, how to be able to live in several dimensions at the same time. She had difficulty in discerning between who was 'I' and who was 'we'. In her soul energy, she was able to feel my male soul energy. This was exciting and rich but also unsettling. She found it helpful to keep busy with worldly things such as doing interviews, travelling to different cities and focusing on the mundane things of life. Through this, we were calibrated even more efficiently with the outer world.

Two commitments reached us through people we had known from our work lives who were inspired from the spiritual world. The idea was that there would be cooperation between worlds working with them. Our soul union had enhanced our ability to influence through healing energies wherever we went. Of course, this happened in the background, inspiring the worldly organisational process work that was accomplished. This is an example of how the spiritual world likes to use what humans have of hands, feet and hearts, as well as their experience and talent.

Travelling between different working places and hotels, B felt how the merging of our souls was now affecting her physical body in a new way. She had surrendered her right part of the physical body to my male soul energy and I was now leading us from my soul. To her, this was a huge surrender and meant that she was leaving her habitual control.

The vulnerability that had always been behind this sense of control was now totally exposed and in the demanding situation of a strong commitment. Still, through the fact that we were so close in our souls and energies, she was able to relax and enjoy herself.

On and off, the energy in her physical body was blocked and she needed to go for walks to help the energy get through. She often experienced a new kind of cold sweat and understood that this was related to the inner processes. On one occasion at the end of a journey, when she had garnered a new kind of security, I played a little with her and she recognised me in that. I wished to challenge her need to use two alarm clocks to wake up in time in the morning, so I made some changes so the clocks didn't work as she expected. She was ready, but unconscious of time when the taxi outside called for her. There was no time for a peaceful breakfast but she was in good time for her work. On her way there, she laughed to herself. The dream I had sent her so she would be in time was about one of the managers that she had interviewed the day before. In the dream he was calling her name. He represented the working day ahead.

Between the trips to work, it was extra wonderful to be able to meet in our own little temple. B was at home with me in our timeless 'soap bubble' that I once had shown her. Our inner marriage in soul meant that we were more or less living in the same frequency, but still in different dimensions. The physical body became our meeting place and our instrument. Through the physical body we were able to experience our soul union and merging, as well as how we together received from the highest light. Kundalini energy flowed through the chakras and feelings of sensuality were lifted to the crown, third eye, heart and the navel chakras, flowing between Heaven & Earth. Several of our clairvoyant friends noticed the change and stated that they felt my presence. A few even saw visual glimpses of me. In our energy bodies we are eternally young, and this is also how I perceive B. All of this created a link to the time when we just had met, had fallen in love with eyes only for each other. We understood that everything of love would merge with what was now happening.

Through our unified flow, the throat chakra was all the more opened. In step with that opening, new inspiration came regarding how to plan for our first book *Love beyond Death*. The consultant work would be a good source of income to finance the publishing of the book, arrange a private book launch and go on a trip after that. Everything was for the best. When this was clear, a distinct image of our books appeared. It was supposed to be a trilogy of three small books instead of a thick one. This meant that the first book was in principle completed, although there was still work to be done. Now the plan appeared to let the book release later during the spring become a party for people close to us, where my presence as soul would be welcomed. It would be a party to celebrate our new life.

The trilogy of books was now clear to both of us. The first book was to be written from B's perspective, while the second book was to be written from my perspective which was made possible through our deepened soul union. I was now able to speak through B. The third book will be created from a perspective beyond both of us. B thought about how it would be possible to write from my perspective and soul. How would that be perceived in the world around us? To us our union has become natural, but to others it might seem strange. On the train on our way home from a travel of consultant work, I spoke to B:

— *The transmission, where you receive me, will be in a way which means that you merge with my soul energy and experience me from inside as has now happened. This is the way my book will be written. We become one by experiencing each other from inside. When you experience me, I will experience you doing that and be a receiver of your/my male power.*

155

Celebrating our new life.

The new life was about to blossom. To B this year had been prophesied for many years as a time when the cycles of her earthly life would come together. It was clear to her that she would either physically die or something cataclysmic would happen. She felt that her intuition had been confirmed; her old life would die and a new kind of life would be manifested. During the years since my passing, the year of 2016 had become more and more distinct. To B, the issue concerned transforming into a totally new identity. This new identity gradually grew into form in step with how our souls were merging. I existed already in the light and had chosen to wait for my soul partner so we could ascend to the highest light together. This was our contribution to the divine plan that concerns all humanity. All souls have their unique contributions.

To B the new identity was about living from the soul while her physical body was still on Earth. When 2016 began, we had reached far in our soul union and we had received lots of light to the physical body. The actual portal to our new life would be to publish our book *Love Beyond Death*. For B, this involved being courageous and daring to stand up for what we have been gifted to experience. To her it would otherwise be more than enough to enjoy and be happy through our soul union. However, in the spiritual world it includes spreading the word further to others who are longing. If due to fear you back off, the flow stops. What we have been gifted to receive belongs to everyone, not only to us. B had made her decision long ago. Now it was about focusing and living to make the flow so strong that it would permeate the remaining inner and outer obstacles.

I made it clear to B that I now was able to and wished to take the lead. She had asked me for help concerning some old thought patterns that were disturbing the flow. As I had so many other times before, I approached her on a train and transmitted to her:

— *We have found each other well after as what I consider a short period of time. I am so happy to have more space. We need that. You have a lot to get used to experiencing me as soul so distinctly. But also to me as soul to get used to being so close and to meet in the physical body. This is great and for us there is a lot to come. We are like pioneers.*

Your thought patterns belong to a fight far beyond life on Earth. We are many and we are linked. To let go of this wider perspective is dangerous. We hold a responsibility that concerns more than just ourselves. Nothing is allowed to divide us and the great power of love we carry within. I tell you this in all seriousness because it concerns strong forces. But now you know. I will take care of us and protect us. It is up to you to keep this wider perspective. Remember that!

The flow increased during the days after our meeting on the train. With my soul energy, I became more firmly established in the physical body, that was perceived as more and more androgynous and where we met through our respective male and female soul energies. Further on, the male and female would be experienced enriched by the many other lives that M and B have lived as souls. This development is necessary to be able to understand what our life task is about. Later, during a walk in nature close to our home, when B was sitting on a bench to enjoy the view over the sea, I transmitted to her:

— *Don´t forget that now we are the syntheses of our incarnations where we have been both man and woman. And now we are both. This you would not find in any books. We are leading. It concerns the ancient fight between the*

159

sexes. We are here to contribute in healing this. In the new era, everything will be united into one. We have had this duality to be able to learn. There are forces that wish to stop this development by trying to divide us. That is why I take the lead now. I have been away from the Earth for a longer time than you and I am freer, so I will be able to protect us.

You already existing on Earth, although identified with your soul and not the person you were in the past, makes us more efficient when it comes to our life task. The reason why I take command today is because we will take a step in our development through me ensuring that we meet close for long periods. Then no attempt to divide us will reach us. No outer threat will succeed. If it becomes too difficult, you might leave life on Earth. But we have a lot to transmit before that can happen, including producing our books and the filling of the physical body with light.

The fact that we exist in our bubble of light is our contribution as we let this love energy spread to the Whole. Those who are open feel the resonance and are enriched by the energy. Recognising is important, as you know.

The writing you are about to do today will be supported by me later this evening. Meeting now in the sunlight is especially nourishing to us. I love you, my little dove!

Some days later I transmitted to B that now we had reached a balance between our soul energies in the physical body. As souls, we met in the physical body as in a trembling midpoint, a zero-point of male and female. It became like a completion and created deep satisfaction in both body and soul. Later that same day, we met in an intense light bubble of energy that embraced us. The heart and the thymus were widened. This time we were led to our special place in the inner world, the place for our soul wedding. The place was the same as before, although this time there was no altar. Instead, a big eye, the all-seeing eye, appeared in the sky. It invoked the feeling of meeting God in this form. Simultaneously, there was a distinct sensation in the forehead of the physical body. These words came to us:

– *Now you have the sign in the forehead. This means that you have accomplished what you have been heading towards for so long. Your lives are complete; your souls are now like one soul.*

We asked what the sign was and were shown a triangle with its peak upwards, a triangle that radiated from an intense light. We asked once more to be quite sure as the same triangle had appeared after our soul wedding. The voice came again:

– *This means that your souls have come to completion. Now you have a choice to make. You decide together. Your intense light might arise a lot in the world around you. This can make living on Earth demanding. M, within you are protecting, but still.*

You might choose to live more in seclusion to be able to live more peacefully while on Earth. Or you might decide to go home. Maybe you will wait until you have published your books. Sometimes, people easier receive this kind of message when there is no physical contact. And you will leave a legacy to humans both known and so far unknown.

The triangle as energy was embodied in the physical body and filled it with extremely high energies. Traces of light flowed through the body and the triangle as light was brought from the forehead out into the body, creating a light triangle over the sex organ with the same intense light as in the forehead. A voice told us:

– *This is a triangle you can turn in all directions. Two through love create a third that is not a duality. This is a gift to the Whole. The duality of Man & Woman is what most people do not want to give up. They don´t understand that there is endless space for everything. You reveal this. Every time you enjoy and are happy with each other, waves go out into the Whole.*

The voice continued:

– *Both your triangles create a star that shines in the night sky. We bless and thank you.*

Carefully and slowly we left this intense light meeting and the meeting with the force of Creation itself. We repeated what the voice had told us so nothing would get lost in meeting with the outer world. The triangle in the forehead returned as a reminder and the voice confirmed:

– *It is important that you remember. Write it down!*

It might seem strange we received this reminder after an experience that was totally revolutionary to both of us. However, experiences in these high energies are subtle and it is essential to shelter them from the noise of Earth. Only afterwards did we remember that we had been invited to a kind of council with the purpose of partaking in these overwhelming perspectives. For B, this was a first glimpse of something beyond comprehension. And she wondered – how is it possible to live with this while still on Earth?

Calibration between our souls

Partly as a joke, I call our meetings with our new spiritual guide an advanced variation of couple therapy between souls. Couple therapy had been a vital part of our professional lives in our last life together. Now it happened to us as souls in our cooperation between the dimensions. As soul on a journey close to the vibrations of the Earth, I needed to express my perspective of what happened. As souls it was new to both of us to meet in one and the same physical body. Understanding that I (even if I had come to the light) was not free from difficulties awoke much tenderness within B. Since my passing, I as soul had existed far away from the noise of the Earth, so I had not been confronted by remaining vulnerabilities. Coming closer to Earth had created uneasiness and a feeling of not being free in the midst of everything that was filled with love.

Understanding that we both held vulnerabilities made it necessary for us to meet with an intense sensitivity to each other´s perspectives. While writing in the diary, we found a way to create written dialogue between our souls. Unexpectedly, we got help from an earlier life. In that life we were king and queen who governed from the highest light. The authority from that life became of great help to us so we could together stand in our light. The weekend after these experiences we had been calibrating ourselves as souls in the same way as we once used to as a physical couple, through dialogue, and I transmitted to B:

— *This weekend has been a kind of breakthrough for us. Through living from each other we have understood what creates unease within each of us. Our love is growing and I feel more safe meeting in the physical body so close to the noise of Earth. We have both journeyed far.*

When we met a moment ago, you invited me to speak. Then inspiration came as a light beam in the neck of the body. That is how we got guidance. The beam passed through the physical body, especially the left side. This created more balance between our souls and I could experience myself as an instrument to send out the message. The triangle was pulsating in the forehead and I/we brought that energy to the united lower triangle. I expressed that we now send this energy as a healing of old wounds between Man and Woman on our Earth. Those who resonate will receive into their lives on their path.

When this ceremony was complete, I told B about the earthly link. Our strength comes from existing in our different dimensions. I showed her that our soul love meetings now always start from the area behind the navel and the uterus. Later, we would meet only in a universal way and that would be more than enough.

The organising of our great party

Our book was now almost complete. It happened through delightful cooperation between close friends, and our son from our latest life together was part of the team. That was a great joy and gave special meaning to us. The day for the book launch was settled. We had decided that the book launch would take the form of a private party for those who had assisted us along our path and for those who were open to our message. It would be a party that would help us say goodbye to our old life and welcome the new. This great transformation would happen with and through about fifty people who were open to my presence as soul.

The beautiful rooms for the party were preliminary booked. B had asked me for help with a certain part of the manuscript that was hard for her to get through. I called her in from daily life and transmitted to her:

— *It concerns our book. You have been reading the manuscript up to a point where you start to censor for the outer world. Now you are aware that our Masters and other light beings are approaching you and us to assist.*

In the midst of our conversation, we received loving help from our Masters and other light beings. At first, Master Sananda approached with his gentle and yet so strong energy and he transmitted:

— *You cannot serve two Masters[4]!*

Then the others came and expressed together with me:

— *You are never alone, never!*

After this intense intervention, B again read through the last part of our book, especially the lines she had been about to censor. Now she was reading with new eyes and deeper understanding. That made her feel pride and joy instead of anxiety as before. She realised that this was because she had expanded her consciousness. The calibration between our souls the weekend before had contributed to this transformation.

The day after I was with her during a meeting she had with colleagues who gave her heartfelt support. She openly shared her anxiety that she had experienced relating to publishing our book and told them what had happened the evening before. Old friendships made it possible to transform anxiety into happy laughter. During the break, she went upstairs to the rooms for the party. Now it was time to confirm the booking and find out about the arrangements.

---

4) This refers to the choice between earthly and spiritual matters

Farewell to the old life

To fully identify yourself with your soul and not with your body or your personality may sound easy, but in practice the transformation is very delicate. To us, on our souls' journey, it meant that I took the lead to ensure that there would be no threat to our soul union. Further on our journey to the light, we would be so calibrated that the issue of leadership would no longer remain. But now was a critical time. During the time up to the book launch, we were in the midst of preparing to say farewell to the old life, the old identification. During our inner dialogue, I transmitted to B:

— *You and I are becoming more and more aligned; it has begun to feel natural and free. We are able to contribute more together and our strength grows. Our book Love Beyond Death is important in this. It gives an outer reason for gathering and having a party, but the party is itself a demonstration of strength. Now you are flying, little dove!*

A new era is now on Earth. Your upcoming birthday is our part of this. Then we will leave the last parts of the old life. The physical body received great help yesterday; I was with you when an old cell memory was released. Everything has happened step by step. In fact, all the cells are to be replaced, so gradually there will be a new body. You felt how we were almost flying home in the car and you saw the special light around us. It will continue like now with further downloading of energy and light.

Finally, you can fully stretch yourself and keep your dignity. For so long, you have allowed people to eat your energy so you became drained. Now that you have fully chosen our path, the answer comes as this enormous flow in the physical body. It also shows in the way we address the world around us.

166

It all happens on a light energy cell level. You feel this in a subtle way through the energy coming in and also through the way the physical body reacts. We meet in new ways. The intellect would never be able to figure out something like this. Everything starts from our unified heart and it flows into our shared light body.

To be able to be on Earth embodying this experience requires that you totally leave the old life, all your old identifications. 'Time to say goodbye' as you heard in the song. You can meet with family and friends, but you cannot be involved in their dynamics and dramas. When we meet our spiritual guide next time, we will have a ceremony where you surrender to me to lead us. There are several reasons for this. Above all, we will be freer and you will rest in nourishing energies. It is about our commitment and our balance as Man & Woman. There is more for me to express on Earth. Some of it will be linked to our next book. The rest will be expressed in other ways.

B answered my transmission with great joy. She was longing to be allowed to let go completely. Some time ago she had researched making a journey to Mallorca after our book launch. We both felt that it would be valuable to have a longer period of time living fully in our own bubble, allowing us the possibility of going deeper. The place was familiar to B as she had been there many times and this would make it easier to focus on our inner life. Also, we felt it was important to link our time there with previous times when Master Kuthumi had guided her as preparation for what was now happening. The decision prompted joy within us at the same time as it gave the spiritual world a sign that we there would create an empty space for co-creation.

167

Some days later the actual surrender, when I took the lead, happened. I transmitted to B:

— I really wish this for you. And I wish to lead us. Now it is time. The total faith you have placed in me is the essence of our love. Now the physical body again is being filled with light that is coming in through the neck and the crown. Maybe it is time to go to bed and let this flow continue all night. We are experiencing a crucial time up to your birthday when we will be filled in a powerful way so the shift will happen. I am happy that you have completed the booking to Mallorca. We will face an intense time and it will continue during the summer. Later, we will have more long periods like this.

Now it is time for me to take over. This is the kind of energy that you felt for a moment just before you went away to meet our grandchild. You also felt this on the way home and do so now at home. I understand that it is radical in relation to the world around you. Impulses you used to have are cut off and my energy is now flowing through the whole physical body.

When I take over, more light flows in as I already exist in the light. Right now your head is filled with energies and you have lost a link to Earth. In the moment you were about to ask about how you in a good way could contribute in the transition, you stopped because the room totally lit up. In that moment, the transition happened.

You told me you felt how everything, all habitual impulses, were suddenly cut off and all was empty. Then the light appeared out of the emptiness. That is how it happens. I am so happy. Now there is no point of return. You have understood this for a long time. I know and feel that you are in wonder.

168

In fact, you have already written about this in our book "Love Beyond Death", saying that you are resting in the arms of my soul while you are living your life on Earth. Now you have reached a deeper understanding. You are my whole world and I enjoy that you now have taken the step that I have been longing for. I wish to hold you, shelter you and welcome you to us here. And I wish to thank you for being able to cut off your old identity while you still exist on Earth.

When the energy of the soul fully is leading life on Earth

The transformational occasion when I as soul took the lead, turned out to be necessary. The closer my soul came to the noise of the Earth, the sharper my reactions became. Simultaneously, B was raised in frequency and was reading my impulses all the more. She had asked me to be precise, as she was longing and wished all the way to live from our soul union, but she needed precise signals from me. Only a few days after I had taken the lead, we visited a group of friends. They were open to their own soul journey and B thought that it would also be a good environment for us. Maybe it was too early, because my soul reacted intensely. In the evening of the same day, we met over our written dialogue and I expressed how I had perceived this meeting. She felt that I was harsh in a new way, listened carefully and at the same time found herself not feeling good enough. The day after, our written dialogue continued:

B: So now it is only you and me.

M: *How wonderful, but the music is distracting.*

B: I agree, I have turned it off now.

M: *You have no idea how it is for me when we get disturbed – like being on a merry-go-round.*

B: I am beginning to understand and also that this is increasing the deeper your soul energy enters the physical body.

M: *So it is. And you are beginning to discern what is distracting.*

B: We can be out together and work in cooperation. That works as long as we get breaks. What is disturbing is when other people's paths take over our own.

M: *Precisely! That is why it is so necessary that you cut off the threads concerning friends and family and that you meet them from the perspective of the soul. Then you will be free to fly.*

B: I am no longer the one who keeps together and balances. But I am able to fly in and out when the timing is right.

M: *We have several days to meet and calibrate ourselves further. We will need this stillness and time. What we go through requires our focus and our ability to meet in high frequencies. It will have great consequences for daily life. You will notice this all the more during the time ahead.*

B: It has great consequences. It is already like that and I understand that I need to be prepared for more.

M: *Little daily things like turning off the TV early in the evening. One or two good programmes are OK. Then it takes over and disturbs.*

B: I have noticed this and also my old habits in the morning and in the evening.

M: *When you tell me this, the light becomes more clear. Old habits are the most difficult to release, but it is important to consider details like these. It is all about making space for what will be created. Otherwise, time will be filled with little habits.*

B: Finally, I really understand you through living from your perspective. Also that it is absurd when I am dealing with a lot of things that are actually unimportant.

M: *You are all the more with me in the light, even physically. We are increasingly one on a soul level and with the physical body. Then you resonate with me and it is wonderful, as well as a perquisite to our path and commitment.*

B: Yesterday evening I almost felt you being harsh, but when today I am reading our dialogue, I do understand.

M: *When the physical body gets too tired, the frequency gets lower. Then it becomes like a merry-go-round to me, so I need to be clear.*

B: And I needed to learn how to discern in time what is happening.

M: *My tenderness is with you! You have been through a lot. From time to time you have looked for confirmation in books and from people who might have experienced something similar. Now we are approaching a new period when you will gradually be able to let go of the last outposts of your old life.*

In this way, we were calibrating us as souls in a deepening way. As time passed, we were more and more in harmony and joy. We listened and lived from the other´s perspective through the slightest detail. Through living from each other, we understood the deepest vulnerabilities within each other. Everything was transformed into love. This is what true love is about and the greatest you can experience as Man & Woman. Our calibration on this uttermost existential level would be a part of our contribution to the Whole. To us it was a matter of life and death. It became evident that the more light filled the physical body, the more caution was needed. Our surrender to each other was total and from a point of no return. Our profound living into each other made it possible. This is the secret of how to create love and peace.

The weeks before B's birthday were filled with consultancy work in the outside world. The work went well and with a greater depth than ever before. We were there together and became more useful through spreading our healing energies. 'Hold the space' is a beautiful expression in English. It was through holding the energies that we contributed the most, even if on the surface it looked like process-oriented consultant work. In this work, our soul brother joined us in a clear way that we both felt.

B's birthday indicated the consequence of leaving the old life. A situation arose that was completely resolved from the perspective of the soul. It was about cutting the ties and putting up necessary boundaries in a way that was foreign to B. During that day, we had been to a session with our spiritual guide. We were strengthened and filled with the energies of the path of our soul union. The challenge later that day turned into a situation to break with the old life's expectations and roles. The following weeks were filled with travel to and from work which helped us stay in our united energy as our foundation in life. Our focus was on our shared journey to the highest light.

The release that resulted from the challenge created an intense energy that was focused on completing the book *Love Beyond Death* and creating a framework for our book launch. Everything found its place and in step with that our own energies were raised more and more. Obviously, this party would be more than a simple book launch. We were eager to gather friends from whom we had got valuable help. These people were working in their own spheres of spiritual work and these spheres seldom meet. However, we felt that this was exactly

172

what was needed. We need to gather to be able to contribute to the healing of our Earth.

Cleansing and healing

There was now barely two months left before our party. During that time, we were raised despite multiple distractions. Through ourselves we learnt what goes for all humanity, how we are linked to each other and how we influence the Whole with ourselves. I transmitted to B:

– *We are linked to a vast universal web of light. We are many souls who together are here to contribute in raising Earth from her heaviness. We are doing this with ourselves and our own lives. There is no other way. That is why it is so much more efficient that you are still on Earth and we meet as souls in the physical body. Through that, we reach deeper. As we are all linked to each other, the whole web of light is affected by all that happens, so when we ascend to the light and are still linked to the Earth, many more will be raised at the same time. Those who right now are not able to receive light will have a hard time. That is why this polarisation is happening now on Earth. It will be even tougher, grotesque and cruel. But everything will be raised to the surface to be healed later.*

You have gradually let go of earthly pleasures. We now enjoy in a different way. And we will enjoy in our way, this delicate bliss that unites our souls with the physical body. We are favoured to experience this. The ways we used to express love in earlier times are still with us; what comes from love never disappears. You tell me that you even now feel our unique essence, the tone of our love, that it is there all the way. It is like that because this part of us never dies. It is eternal. Through our love for each other, we are born into the higher frequencies. We create this through our love.

When there was one month left to our party, we had lived through what was once my birthday and two days after that the day of my passing. To both of us as souls it was clear that it was time to leave memory and celebration days from our old life. Instead, through our party we would celebrate our new life together with friends who could embrace us as souls. I transmitted to B:

– *We are free now and we are the same energy. You experience disturbances of the energy flow in the same way as I do. Now you feel how the blue light is filling the physical body. It is Christ energy, pure love. We are raised all the more. The heart of ruby that you many years ago resonated so strongly with is about this kind of love. Your/ our jewellery is there as a symbol of this love. And now the bracelet will be on the cover of our book Love Beyond Death so the book will resonate in this energy. The other books will follow in step with how we journey on our path to the highest light. All is happening in parallel. We are now approaching the state of consciousness when it will be possible to create the next book. We needed to be raised to where we are now to make it possible. And we will be raised further during the actual work. We have a wonderful time ahead of us.*

While this was happening, Easter was approaching and on Easter Day there was a new important step. We knew that there was no point of return on our souls' journey. Still, a part of the journey included that B once more was asked to make a choice from her innermost essence. This happened during one of our meetings, when we as souls were flying away and felt how all threads to the Earth were gone. B showed this with her left arm that in our meeting turned into a wing. She was waving with her wing to the Earth and was flying into my soul arms. We were flying high up. It was so beautiful around us.

174

When we had landed from our flying tour, we told each other through our written dialogue:

B: Finally totally free. Not even old thoughts are able to reach me. I could and can now see where we are and I feel as if you are holding your right arm around me. Forever.

M: *This last step you needed to take from your innermost will. I have been using my spiritual sword to cut threads. This was your step and now you have taken it. A step in line with Easter day, don´t you think?*

B: It began with this zero point when all identities disappeared and dissolved and melted together. 'We' now meant being at one with everything. Then it was finally possible for me to let go.

M: *The zero point is exactly that – beyond all identities we have ever had. We can fly away and we can meet in the physical body that is still on Earth.*

Through the zero point and our flying tour far beyond Earth, we had reached an important step. After that it was time for the physical body to receive extensive cleansing. This resulted in fever, an ice-cold shivering that to the world around took the shape of a heavy flu. To us it was obvious that it was the light that had been flowing through old layers. When this happens, old 'goo', old destructive forces, are burnt both from within and without. I transmitted to B:

– *The energies, the light that turns into fever, are cleansing all that is projected on to us, the physical body. These energies get burnt by the light. Living in these energies in this time on Earth is hard. But every soul has its own path to follow.*

We are now preparing for the next step that in the outer world will be manifested through our book launch. But so much more is happening on our journey to the light. To the physical body it is a lot to bear. We just have to live through this.

Old memories that create blockages in the body must leave as we fly higher. Or rather, the more light that comes into the cells, the more old heaviness must disappear. It always comes after you have made your decisions and taken your steps. Everything is fine. The fact that it happens in such an intense way now shows how much light we have been gifted to receive in the physical body.

My energy will influence the physical body more in the time ahead of us. Our body needs different energy flows at different times. After the book launch, we will focus on our next book: "Union of Souls". You will write this book from your living into my soul. It will not be a traditional channelling, it will be unique to your path. That is why my energy will be stronger as long as it is needed.

Do you hear the birds outside? Our united soul is there while the physical body is struggling with letting go of the old. When it enters sleep or dormancy, it is filled with light.

Now we are filling the physical body with our soul energies of which the male will dominate for some time. I am getting used to this as are you. I am excited and full of desire for our journey together. We are building the energy for the next step, beginning with the book launch and the manifestation it includes. Then Mallorca. There are so many threads and we are many souls weaving together. We are aligned with the coming spring and will blossom in the same way.

The portal to our new life, in the shape of our book launch, became the gathering of forces that we had been shown. Fifty people came together in a meeting from the heart, sharing the longing to contribute to a more peaceful world. My presence was natural to those who were there. B spoke to them and told our story about *Love Beyond Death* and we were received with warmth and appreciation. A friend of us created a framework from song and music that was in resonance with the message. Even as soul without body I could enjoy that we were located in a beautiful environment and that the guests enjoyed nice food and drink. All parts of life were to be celebrated.

Before and after this great day, I as soul went through crucial events affecting us both. Through these occasions, I let go of old earthly threads. The development of our souls continues after our passing. My increased freedom made me as soul ready to come even closer to the energy field of Earth.

Spring has never been as brilliant

After our book launch, spring budded into full bloom. It was like a reflection of the blooming of our souls in the union that we now had been living in for so long. The calibration between our souls implied that the physical body was receiving all the more light into its cells. It felt lighter and more ethereal and B was raised in energy.

The higher into the light we as united souls flew, the closer to the noise of the Earth my soul energy could exist. This created an experience of meeting in the same physical body with total living from each other´s soul.

The month of May brought great experiences every day, with the feeling of being together and receiving the spring from two energy sources through the physical body. We received the heavenly perspective as well as the earthly. Simultaneously, we became both sender and receiver for each other in an endless chain of intense moments.

We often visited cafés, sitting where possible outside. B did the writing and M channelled the words for the new diary. This was part of the preparation for our book *Union of Souls* from the perspective of my aspect of our united energy field. Being a soul without a physical body, it was an unimaginable feeling to have the opportunity to speak in this way. Throughout the years, I had spoken to B many times, so we were used to our inner conversations. Now it was time for me to speak to the world from my current perspective. When we met clairvoyants, the three of us talked together – to me these were solemn occasions. After spring had passed, some of our other friends felt my presence and we talked together. When they were open to it, it happened in a natural way. They noticed a different energy if the voice came from my soul energy or from B.

This chapter includes examples of the occasions when I spoke through B's pen. We both felt that it was another energy coming through, and that this was more evident when I was speaking as one flow and not in dialogue with B. Still, the most important factor was that we now both were more free to affirm the great gift we had been given. As reader, you will now be part of the language of our daily inner conversations. Reading this book, you will understand that the conversations are between us as souls and that our united soul energies have gradually been calibrated with the energies of the physical body.

Our souls are merging

– *My little darling! Thank you for your loving way of receiving me in our united soul energy that is now filling your body! It is possible now because you yourself are identified in soul and not with the physical body. You have surrendered it to our shared journey in soul. What we are experiencing belongs to the great mysteries of life. It is impossible to understand from your intellect.*

The heart and the soul hold this wisdom. How you understand depends totally on your state of consciousness. You limit yourself when you believe that a human being only has five senses and an intellect created by the brain itself. When we realise we are multi-dimensional beings, new worlds open to us.

When I was living on Earth, I alternated between ease in experiencing other worlds and dimensions to on the other hand letting my intellect take over. My intellect was not able to embrace what I a moment before had experienced as real, so I defined it as just an inner emotional experience. Those were the moments when I said to you: 'Do you have to be that concrete?'

The moment arrived, thanks to support and preparation, when we in an inner ceremony with our Masters were married in soul. From that moment, our united soul energy was allowed to live in your physical body. Several steps were and are needed to complete this. Simultaneously, the body is filled with more light.

There have been forces that wished to prohibit our merging as souls. We have been tested and now we are free. All has happened in love and light and with the assistance of our light friends both on Earth and on this side. That is why we begin a new diary today. I come to you today to show you how our life will unfold from now on. The struggle is over. Now we will meet in light and energy during both day and night.

Remember what Master Kuthumi told you ten years ago. All the openings of the physical body remain in a refined form in the seven bodies[5]. This means we are expressing ourselves to each other as Man & Woman, but the expressions are different from the physical.

All that we have experienced of love during our life together on Earth, as well as during other lives, is now with us when we meet in soul. That is why we don't lack anything now. We bring with us all of love while we travel to the light receiving even more from the mysteries of life.

We in the Whole

We have beautiful days together now. Life has become calm and peaceful. You tell about us in small doses and we are well received. We need a lot of time and our own focus. What we are going through is greater and more radical than is possible to embrace from an earthly perspective.

---

5) Referring to the Seven Energy Bodies

We are linked to other souls in an ingenious way in which we are all dependent on each other. That is why it is so important that we fulfil our own roles.

It is not about time in the way you think on Earth. Time and space don´t exist where I am now. It is more like widening qualities that lift us to the light. When we are able to embrace darkness with light, everything expands. It creates a chain reaction and affects everything. That is how we influence the Whole, through ourselves.

Hologram: when you understand the hologram, you understand the Universe. In every part is the Whole. When one part embraces worry and fear, love then surges through the Whole. That is why meeting in groups from the heart is so powerful.

Our new life will unfold in a similar way. We will become more a powerful love magnet the higher in frequency we reach. We unite Heaven & Earth and Man & Woman. As you many times have drawn in your diary, it appears as the symbol of a like sided cross with a significant point in the middle where everything unites.

Do you notice that the words come in a slightly different way now that you have given the word to me? It was a good idea to do the transition by dialogue. Still, it is different now that you allow me to take this role. The energy is clearer and more directed. And you are living into being my essence in our united soul energy. That is how my expressions and uniqueness have become more apparent.

What we are doing in this way will be the foundation for Union of Souls. We practice here at home and prepare ourselves. Later in Mallorca, we will stay in this flow day and night. Then we will reach even deeper. I feel that we are both experiencing joy and excitement in this new flow. Neither of us know what might appear. We just stay open.

We will be in the flow and do the editing afterwards, like you did with the other books. It is a good approach that makes us free.

I notice that you are longing to go to bed. During the night is the time when we really fly. You don´t remember all these flying tours. We visit other planets and places in the Universe, and we contribute on Earth and hold the energy where needed. We unite places and energies with ourselves as instrument.

Nature and us

We are so close to each other on this wonderful early summer day. Heaven & Earth meet when nature awakens. And the birds are giving us a concert. Through our soul union, all the more now this union also is embodied in the physical body, I gain a unique opportunity to experience the earthly from a heavenly perspective. And you all the more get access to my perspective, although you remain on Earth.

We have received this gift so we can show the way and share that this is a possibility for everyone. I understand that this is a challenge to you. Most people find it strange, and some even distance themselves from it. But there are many who one way or another recognise themselves and are longing. Have faith that everything will work out in a natural way! Yesterday, when we went for a trip that included some time on a car ferry, my experience became especially strong and close to the physical. And you gained the experience of being a man sitting by the steering wheel in a line of cars on a ferry.

Living from each other is a crucial key of our love and it travels with us in the development of our soul union. This is the highest aspect of love between Man & Woman. We are merging the polarities through mutual living into each other. This is not a melting together of an earthly kind, when you no longer exist as separate beings. Rather, it happens due to us being raised in frequency, to a higher light, where there is space for both and where we become whole through living from both our own and each other's perspectives. All of humanity will gradually develop in the same way.

Now I, who on Earth always was longing to be free, experience this high aspect of both freedom and love. The two are linked. You cannot love without being free and you cannot be free without being able to love.

When you are sitting in your armchair writing my words, I am like one with you. Through your eyes I enjoy the blue sky and the buds of the trees. Through your ears I hear the birds singing. And through your heart I become filled with joy and happiness. My part of our soul union gives you signals through the light pillar and our united light bodies. Simultaneously, with your sensitive body awareness, I experience how the energies are moving in your body, which all the more is felt as ours.

You have welcomed me to this wonder. I have welcomed you to be embraced by me while you are still on Earth. We are now in a calmer phase. We are being embraced by the light together. Destructive forces aren't reaching us any more. Love embraces everything.

We meet in emptiness

You give this emptiness to us, and at once we meet in the light pillar, the energies come in waves. Through your body and senses, I experience the verdant spring in a particularly strong way and I feel that it is the same for you.

Your body has become more ethereal. We go to the light that comes into the body and is filling the cells. This means that you too receive the spring stronger than ever. You have become calm now, and that to me is very pleasant. The stress and worries of Earth don´t reach you as before. You have moved into me and I have moved into you. Through that, we are sheltered and keep on calibrating ourselves on our journey to the highest light.

Our home is our temple and platform for our new life together. We received this gift as a part of developing our new life, our shared life task. Those who come to our home, feel and accept my presence there. One or two friends at a time is enough.

The song of the birds are lifting us and others in these times. From Master Kuthumi you learnt to let the song of the birds show the way so your soul can fly. You and I have met like that a couple of times. We met there in endless love and endless freedom. You were able to feel my presence when we as souls were flying beside each other.

Now we are living this every day. When I passed over, my inner image was that I would return to the peace in Tibet. Instead, this great gift was granted and I realised that you and I are on a shared journey in soul. With wonder, joy and gratitude I received this gift. I understood that the freedom that I during my life as Mikael had been guarding fiercely, does not exist without love. That love does not exist without freedom. That is why what we are experiencing is such great grace.

As souls we continue to mature both here and on Earth, but it happens in slightly different ways. Doing this, you and I together with the perspectives of both Earth and Heaven, is a great wonder. I feel great tenderness towards you who remain on Earth, and need to relate to this at the same time as we develop and are developed through our marriage in soul.

186

At first, you did not understand that I was always with you. Time does not exist here. I was able to dock with you when you were open to it. These were solemn occasions to me, and to you it became more and more evident that there is no separation other than in the thoughts you create on Earth.

From my perspective it is incomprehensible how most people on Earth spend much of their time running around in circles. They do it in thought and in action, and this fills their lives. There is much more to tell about how we have come to the state of consciousness we now are sharing. Enough for today of looking back.

The important thing is where we are now. Through your ears I hear families and small children talking outside. They are busy with their daily lives. There is much of life in this and once we were there as well. Different kinds of joy. Every time has its meaning. Now you and I have the resource of deepening within the great mysteries of existence. And we are doing this through ourselves and our united souls. This is an endless journey that we both have wished for and longed for during eons of time. Whatever time is.

Our meetings then and now

You noticed that I in energy took over the steering wheel coming here. Now you understand more of how this is happening. When our united soul energy is moving into your old physical body and it gets filled with light, I gain access to your eyes, ears and other senses. It is awesome to be able to experience it in this way. Now it works very well. We have been calibrating and now we are in tune with each other. Walking from the car, the legs were in pain, this time especially the right one. You continued

187

walking –that was good. Just before the café, the energies came through and the leg collapsed a bit. All went well and it is much softer now. Our soul journey requires a lot of your physical body. It has been stiff and unbalanced. Gradually, as the light comes in and we are raised in our union, the stiffness and the imbalance will disappear and the body will become free. In the meantime, it is valuable, to get help so you keep your mobility.

We meet like in an energy bubble many times throughout the day and during the night. Yesterday it was like that as soon as you had finished watching TV and eating your dinner. Then I came to you in our light pillar. You felt the heat in your lower back. Every such light meeting is at the same time our gift to the Whole. We enjoy and contribute simultaneously. This is how Universe is created! Actually, I have always understood this, even when I was living on Earth as Mikael.

You have acquired new habits or rather let go of routines. This is good for us. Now we first meet and the outer world comes later. Yesterday, we consciously met several times in our bubble. I am always within you, whatever you do. But when we consciously meet in our bubble, we are at the same time filled with light. Yesterday we continued and let the light come into every nook and cranny of the body. All will be one and it happens gradually.

There was a period of time when you told me several times each day: 'Now I am entering you and we are lifted together.' At the same time, you were sheltered from some of the challenges on Earth. That is how it happens. We have been welcoming each other into our most secret rooms. Love makes it possible. Freedom and love, as I mentioned yesterday.

Shortly after my passing, I invited you to merge with my soul energy. Even if we between lives on Earth, had made our agreements, there is always free will to choose anew in every now. You received me with your whole being, even if you also were afraid. It takes courage to live like this on Earth, to go public as you did with our first book. You have made this choice and so we are able to continue our soul journey. There have been many challenges along the path. Now we are through and we can enjoy and rejoice on our soul journey.

When it was time for our united souls to move into your physical body and feel it as ours, the next step began. You welcomed me as soul energy into your physical body and we had a time of calibration that was demanding for both of us. Through conversation and even more living from each other, we journeyed further. Now your struggle with the earthly is over. You were embraced by me and the light my soul brings. Finally, you were able to let go.

Planet Earth

You are arranging daily life so it becomes nice and pleasant to us and I am with you. It is like riding a tandem. This means that we are able to enjoy each other and the beauty now happening on Earth. We experience it from the perspectives of the soul and of love. This gives even more lustre to the colours of the spring and to the singing of the birds.

The gift that we are now living will be given to all human beings. Every soul has its own speed and its own journey. There are older and younger souls. Through many lives we collect experience and wisdom, and then one day it is time to harvest. It is not possible to think about this in an earthly way. It is definitely not about reaching some kind of finishing line as is the case so often on Earth.

Every step in the development of the soul is valuable and enriching. Everything is in movement and flows. It is so beautiful when we are able to embrace the whole picture. That is why every action, thought and feeling surges into the Whole. We are all aspects of each other and still unique. When human beings meet in freedom and love, the whole of humanity is touched.

Through our total surrender to each other we have received a great gift – to have access to both Heaven & Earth. We exist in each other and that is how we become whole. That is how this kind of melding together as souls happen. The keys are love and freedom. I now understand why we as humans have free will and choice. Love cannot exist without this freedom. And there is no gain from free choice without love. Living from each other, welcoming and surrendering to each other is an expression of this freedom and love. This is how it happens.

On Earth there is much violence and wars. Many people lack love and are unable to handle their free will. Far too many dare not receive love and become forever hungry and frustrated. Some are able to receive, and through that mature. We, who have the gift of receiving love, can contribute in different ways. It is not always about helping in a concrete way, even if that also is needed. We have different tasks in different lives and in various stages of a life.

For a long time you have received the image of the lights on planet Earth. This is also a way to contribute by letting these lights meet, connect and strengthen each other. This is above all how we contribute in these times and in this stage of our life – our souls' journey. When we through ourselves unite Heaven & Earth and Man & Woman, this energy, this light, flows into the web of light. Those who resonate with this light are raised with us. Other souls resist now but might choose differently later on. Everyone chooses their own timing.

Our trilogy of books

After this lovesome spring described in this chapter, we made two more travels. The purpose of these was to create the empty spaces that make our deepening possible. Before summer, we went to Mallorca and were in seclusion for twelve days. While travelling, we opened ourselves to let in all previous incarnations to our shared consciousness, all incarnations that could contribute to our soul journey. This process was interwoven with those earlier occasions when B, in the same place, had received her preparations for what is now happening. Through this intense time in stillness, we were raised into higher dimensions.

Later, during the winter, we went to Kerala in India and lived at an ashram for more than six weeks. This time the focus was on helping the physical body to receive our soul energies all the way through. It included our souls letting go of the final obstacles. Among other things, we were assisted by an intense Ayurveda treatment. Back in Sweden, we needed the same amount of time as the actual journey to reach a balance between soul and body. When that happened, we were ready to write this book.

To fully be able to understand what we have been through, we need to continue our soul journey to the highest light. This is how our third book will be created – through ourselves. When we have travelled further on our soul journey, we will have widened perspectives of everything we experienced in Mallorca, India and the times between and after. That book, the third of our trilogy, will be written from an aspect beyond both M and B. Much further on, when we have reached the state of consciousness of that aspect, we will able to write that book. We are already looking forward to it.

Thank you for being
with us on our
journey this far!

EPILOGUE

As Barbro I thank Mikael´s soul for this book! In earthly time the story covers the first five years after his passing. He wished to transmit a lot from his perspective beyond the earthly one. I felt his excitement and joy with all my being. While travelling my path, I have often wondered how this would unfold and struggled with whether it would be possible. My inner guidance has from the beginning been clear that I was supposed to write and that my writing was a part of the beautiful soul journey that I/we have been gifted. I have chosen to say yes and by that also accepted I must face my fears along the path. To confront and conquer these fears turned out to be as important as the actual writing of the books, which became like portals for me to be raised to the light.

My own wonder, concerning what happened during what is described in the book, makes me fully understand that you as the reader might find it difficult to follow the text. The best way would be to (for a while) let go of the logic of the intellect and invite your heart and intuition. That is what I needed to do to accept and live with the course of events.

Every soul journey is unique when it comes to content, expression and symbols. However, there are phenomena along the path that we share. We are all on our way to become one with our inner light. This light I call the 'divine spark' or the 'divine part' that exists within every human being. Within our inner light, humanity is one and the same.

The union of souls is included in every soul's journey. As I wrote in the prologue, this happens every time we pray, meditate or experience a moment of stillness in nature. When we understand that all is energy, it becomes more natural to allow our souls to merge and to live from this union. Many humans experience contact and union with Masters and Angels. For me it also included the experience of merging with the soul of my husband, a union that exists everywhere.

To you, the reader, it might be easier to follow what is told in this book if you have read my other two books, especially *Love Beyond Death*. To make it easier, I have described certain words and concepts in a separate chapter. In the actual story, the chapters express themes that have been crucial to our soul journey. These themes were important but simultaneously they created a dilemma in relation to the time line. Because of that, sometimes an outer journey might be mentioned several times but with different themes in mind. The experience and the learning in itself is the important thing. To me all the (outer) journeys helped me to be able to let go of my habitual way of living and be able to receive the new life in all its beauty.

I hope our story will inspire you and help you to recognise your own soul journey. No soul journey is like any other. Our differences are necessary so together we will become stronger and reach out more. While editing the manuscript I met a close friend, who experienced his soul journey quite differently to how I did. His path is not as kinaesthetic as mine. Instead, he developed a structured practice of stillness and meditation. His path has led to the same kind of joy to meet in the light. We share and respect each other´s path.

Throughout the book you find that I have looked for and got support from friends who have clairvoyant abilities that I don´t possess. Their soul journeys are different to mine and they have meant a lot to me along my path. I used to need their confirmation from outside to be able to trust my own sensations in the body and in the words that I received from the realms of the soul and spirit. They experienced visually what came to me in other ways. I wish to give you these examples so you will recognise how your own path is expressed. When we meet within our differences, we simultaneously deepen our soul journeys. My gratitude is great to this communion in soul while living here on Earth.

BACKGROUND TO WORDS AND CONCEPTS

The view of life that permeates this book, comes from within. As Barbro, during a long life of personal and soul development, I have encountered many symbols and phenomena. I believe that these arise from ancient memories from previous lives that are activated when time is ripe. A special kind of charge was growing that created my excitement and understanding to deepen. Just in time books came my way, books that gave recognition and inspiration and opened me to new worlds. These books became a crucial link to a multidimensional world and to other souls that had explored this path long before. Some of these books are included in the literature list.

My view of life in essence is that there is a divine spark, a divine part in every human being. As souls we come to Earth to develop and grow. We need many lives here and also in other places in Universe to make contact with and become one with our divine part. Within our divine part, all humanity is the same Spirit, while we as souls are individual.

As souls we are linked to each other and we contribute in different ways towards one another's development. The unique tone or essence that every soul has stays with us on our path to the Spirit. All of love stays. There is space as our consciousness expands and we are raised in frequency.

Words and concepts on this list might give you inspiration. However, your own experience is necessary to give meaning. Personally, I had no knowledge of the ascended Masters until Master Kuthumi appeared on my path. In my younger years I worked a lot with body therapy, so I knew the concepts of the chakra system and the kundalini force. I had a vague understanding about the subtle flows in the physical body. Still, it was not until the kundalini force spontaneously broke through in my own body that I fully understood.

A crucial platform for my soul's journey has been the ancient Egyptian mythology, expressed through contemporary mystics. Some of it is shared through this book, but it had started already the year before Mikael and I met as a physical couple. It was already obvious that Mikael came from another spiritual tradition having lived many lives in Tibet. Once when we were meditating together, I saw a monk behind him. His face was warm and loving, his eyes were twinkling and he was smiling humorously.

In the text you will find underlined words that need explanation. All these words are collected in the Words and Concepts chapter. Where possible, I also refer you to books that have helped me understand these words and concepts. I hope that this information will bring joy, recognition and inspiration.

Note: My inspiration comes from the actual books/literature that I have mentioned. I have not met any of the authors in person in their practice, so in that capacity I am not able to advice.

If you are looking for personal and soul guidance, I suggest you choose very carefully. A good sign is when you are met with respect, honesty and care, besides the talents you look for.

WORDS AND CONCEPTS

Ascended Masters: The concept of Ascended Masters comes from Theosophy, a spiritual movement that came into being at the end of the nineteenth century. They are described as enlightened beings who have lived many incarnations on Earth. They are Masters of ancient wisdom and have chosen to assist Earth and humanity in their development. The Masters have their special fields, areas of development that they deepen and protect.

Bliss: The gift of living in high loving energies.

Chakra system: The most well-known chakra system describes seven or eight chakras, but there are also smaller chakras spread all over the body. A chakra is like an energy whirl where the more subtle energies flow within and close to the physical body. The endocrine glands are the link to the physical body. The three lower chakras *root chakra* (physical survival), *sexual chakra* (breeding) and *solar plexus* (maintaining own power) relate to survival as physical individuals. These chakras are powerful and life-giving but need to be governed by the other four. These are the *heart chakra* (love), *throat chakra* (express to the world), *third eye* (to see beyond) and *crown chakra* (divine wisdom). The chakras hold energy of different frequencies.

See *The Human Aura. How to Activate and Energise your Auras and Chakras*, Kuthumi and Djwal Kul.

Chakra system - the Egyptian: The most well-known chakra system describes that we have access to seven or eight chakras. It can be compared to a musical octave. The Egyptian system has twelve or thirteen chakras, where the thirteenth is the first and the last. Drunvalo Melchizedek compares this with the chromatic scale (the thirteen half steps in a musical octave: all the keys on a piano in an octave, including the black ones). I recognised myself in the Egyptian system, as they there speak of two heart chakras, one for universal and one for personal love. It was of great help in understanding what happened when I met Mikael's soul after his passing.

See *The Ancient Secret of the Flower of Life, Volume 2* by Drunvalo Melchizedek.

Cosmic family: The concept of cosmic family has been coined to describe that we as souls often incarnate in groups. Within such a group, there is a belonging concerning type of energy and life task within the divine plan. These souls often also share a common focus in their way of contributing to the development of the Earth. Some people speak of different rays that are described in colours while others speak of groups linked to the ascended Masters.

The Creation and Source: There are many words to describe the divine and the divine aspect of the soul. These are two of them.

Dimensions: Dimensions are linked to states of consciousness and frequencies of energy. In the third dimension, the one that the Earth mostly is imprinted by, we live in a certain belt of frequency of time and space. When meditating, we are raised in energy and enter another state of consciousness with a higher frequency. During our soul journey, we are raised to the higher energies and experience our existence from a totally different perspective. The purpose of the soul journey is to gradually embody all dimensions with the highest, timeless and eternal of which we all are a part.

Divine plan: This book implies and transmits that there is a divine plan to which all humanity belongs. From this point of view, every soul has a life task within this plan. We remember this task between lives, but we often forget it when we come to the Earth. A person's life task might unfold at first in glimpses, but if you focus it becomes more and more apparent. You understand through an experience of resonance with certain situations and happenings. Gradually, as the soul is raised in frequency, your life task unfolds and gives meaning to life. While this is happening, you often make contact with your soul group and find a deeper connection between these souls. The inner picture gets clearer and you understand what you together are meant to do to contribute towards the healing and development of the Earth.

Earth energy: Everything is energy and we are all parts of this common energy. This bigger picture is hard to embrace with the human intellect. Through our subtle energy bodies we as humans are in close contact with the entire cosmos and all energies. To be able to live on Earth, we are totally dependent on being in balance with these forces. The strongest link to these forces is the subtle bodies. However, the physical body is in turn dependent on these energy bodies to be able to live a stable life on Earth. When you consciously open up to your soul journey, it is especially important to make sure that all bodies are in balance. During certain intense periods of time, imbalance often appears. That is why it is so important to look after your physical body while your soul journey continues. To us humans, nature is a valuable source of nourishment.

Egyptian mythology: Ancient Egyptian mythology had a great influence on Christianity and Judaism. Mystics of today have traced knowledge and inspiration from the ancient Egyptian spiritual tradition and created a modern system to understand this.

See *The Nine Eyes of Light* by Padma Aon Prakasha, *The Ancient Flower of Life, volume 2* by Drunvalo Melchizedek and *Anna Grandmother of Jesus* by Claire Heartsong

200

Esoteric: In ancient times, mystery schools were created in which deeper understanding was taught of what otherwise was manifested as religion. Religions are imprinted by the cultures in which they arise while esoteric teaching concerns the inner wisdom behind them. The mystery schools addressed smaller groups working with distinct stages of development manifested as initiations. In that way, it was possible to hide the message so it would not be diluted or in other ways be destroyed.

Etheric school: The ascended Masters have created inner schools that we as souls have access to while the physical body is asleep. You might visualise this as gatherings of energy that works as a kind of education for soul travel. At an early stage I (as Barbro) was guided to the etherical school of Master Kuthumi. I was woken every night, took notes and slept before daily life took over. This took place every night for several years.

Frequency of energy: Frequency of energy is about different speeds of energy and is linked to different dimensions and states of consciousness. Energy is received by us humans as sensations in the body, images or sounds. The book speaks of calibration between souls, calibration of energies concerning frequencies. Lower speeds of energies are embraced by higher energies and the lower energies are raised in frequency. Energies lower when we as humans face fear expressed, for example, as doubt, worry, envy or anger. The energies are raised when we are filled with trust, love and light.

Go to the light: This is an expression that is often used and in a somewhat careless way. In this book the highest light is the same as Spirit, Source, linked to the divine part of each soul where we all are one. We gradually bring in this light that is our divine part. This means that we are more and more filled with light and are all the more able to embrace our divine part. That is what the journey of the soul is about. Even when we after our passing have come to the light, the journey continues to the highest light and beyond.

Goddess Isis: Isis is the mother goddess within the Egyptian mythology and spiritual practice. Her myth describes how Isis after her husband Osiris died collected his fragments and how they together created Horus as their child and simultaneously a god of love. Transferred into spiritual practice, you might view (this as) how Horus is born as a new state of consciousness after Isis (the female) and Osiris (the male) have melded. There are parallels linked to Christ and Christ energy in the way of viewing spiritual development.

201

Incarnate/incarnation: This book implies a view of life where souls are maturing through returning to the Earth and other places in Universe to gather wisdom. The divine part of the individual soul is intact, undestroyable and eternal. The soul journey concerns (in a conscious way) returning to this part that most people so far only are in contact with in glimpses. We incarnate mostly in groups of souls with the aim of assisting each other, often through an apparent support but also in other ways through being part of the challenges.

Initiation: In the ancient mystery schools every new stage meant an initiation that was preceded by concrete challenges that you had to meet. Taken literally, the word 'initiation' means you have taken a step that is not possible to return from. In spiritual life today, the word initiation means a step of decisive importance that includes an inner choice and vow that you cannot change. Future challenges are parts of this inner choice as well as the free will of humanity.

Inner wedding: This concept is a symbol for a soul journey when male and female energies within an individual are united in love. This is a practice that builds on a further development of the kundalini force.

In today´s practice of Egyptian mythology it is called the *Path of Horus*. When you choose the Path of Horus, the sexual energy/life energy within the individual is refined and raised. Another application is called the *Magic Path of Isis* where a loving couple surrender together to transform their sexual energy into higher energies.

See *The Magdalen Manuscript* by Tom Kenyon and Judi Sion.

Kundalini energy: The potential for this energy exists in every human being and is described as being dormant in the lower back to be awoken when time is right. Kundalini yoga is a practice that inspires the kundalini power to awaken. If it wakes too early and you are not yet ready to receive this force, this can create problems. It takes with it everything in its path but gives a hundredfold back. As Barbro, I'd had decades of body therapy and other kinds of therapy when the kundalini force – about twelve years before writing this book – spontaneously broke through. After that, this energy became a concrete guide on my soul journey.

See *Womb Wisdom* by Anaiya Aon Prakasha and *The Magdalen Manuscript* by Tom Kenyon and Judi Sion

Light beings: A light being can be an angel or an ascended Master. In a wider sense, you might use this word for different beings living in the light.

Light body: The light body is a concept within several spiritual paths. Some call it the 'esoteric body'. Within the ancient Egyptian mystery schools, the light body is named *Mer-Ka-Ba*. It describes how to develop a flow of energy and light that weave together the physical body and dimension with other dimensions. This happens through meditation linked to the kundalini force and the different chakras that rest within us humans as a potential. Within Egyptian mythology, Ka is the energy body that is closest to the physical body and simultaneously is linked to Ba, the soul, that in turn is linked to several higher energy bodies.

See *The Nine Eyes of Light* by Padma Aon Prakasha and *The Ancient Flower of Life, Volume 2* by Drunvalo Melchizedek.

Man & Woman and Heaven & Earth: In this book, these concepts concern forces/energies that live and influence every human being, all of nature and the entire cosmos. That is why they are capitalised. Through different incarnations, the soul acquires the potential to experience the earthly existence from a physical body of a man and a woman and with different expressions of sexuality. Through being schooled on Earth, the soul collects wisdom.

Master Kuthumi: Master Kuthumi is one of the ascended Masters. His special focus is love and wisdom. To me/us, Master Kuthumi has been the one who has given us education. Early on my conscious spiritual path, I (as Barbro) was awoken every night over several years and was welcomed to his etheric school. Furthermore, in transition times of my soul journey, he has given transmissions. I/we belong to his cosmic family where we share a special purpose of how we wish to be a part of the divine plan for the development of humanity.

See *The Human Aura* by Kuthumi and Djwal Kul and *Teachings for The New Golden Age* by Kuthumi.

Master Sananda: Jesus Christ is named Sananda as an ascended Master. I (as Barbro) experience Master Sananda as a unique kind of energy – Christ energy. This energy is extremely soft and loving at the same time as its force permeates the darkest dark and light it up. He is present with his crystal energy, Christ energy, at the hardest times of life.

Mother Earth: The concept of Mother Earth is used primarily when you view the Earth as a spiritual being with its own energy. This is also a way to make visible and receive her great love that comes deeply from within and is linked to other expressions of motherly love. Many feel a strong identification with Mother Earth and how badly we humans have been treating her. Through understanding that she is a being of her own, we might as humans realise our responsibility.

Seven energy bodies: During a transmission to me as Barbro, Master Kuthumi related that all openings in the physical body have their parallel in the more subtle energy bodies (bodies of higher frequencies). This means sensations in the physical body but in a more refined, deeper and subtle way.

See *The Nine Eyes of Light* by Padma Aon Prakasha.

Spirit and Soul: In a general sense, these concepts are used in quite a confusing way. They are also used slightly differently in English and Swedish. To many, God is the same as Spirit. The soul is the individual aspect of Spirit and holds a divine part, a spark of the divine. As human beings we have a personality that is our expression on Earth. The journey that humans are making towards God (the Creation, Source) happens only through letting go of the personality as their identification and instead identifying with the soul. The journey of the soul relates to how it more and more makes contact with its divine part and identifies with it. When we as humans are identified with the divine part of the soul, we experience a state of consciousness of being one.

Subtle energy bodies: This concept is used to describe the channels of energy that the physical body is linked to. They are described in books (for instance) about acupuncture and acupressure. They are also linked to the kundalini force and the light pillar that flows through the physical body when this energy has broken free. Derived from the Egyptian tradition are different energy bodies that are linked to each other.

- *Khat/Aufu:* The physical body and its link to the Earth and the Light
- *Ka:* Individual light body that is a link between the physical body and the soul (*Ba*)
- *Shew:* The shadow as a portal to the Source
- *Ren:* The field of vibrations, sounds and perception
- *Ab:* The human heart, the longing and intelligence of the heart
- *Ba:* The soul and the Divine child. The link between the individual and the Universal soul
- *Sekhem:* Life force, bliss and the lightening fire of love
- *Sahu:* The eternal body where you embody the light
- *Akhu:* The consciousness of God that shines through all other light bodies

Padma Aon Prakasha describes these energy bodies as different eyes or lenses. It is a way for us to describe humans as multidimensional beings where the different aspects of us work as a hologram.
See *The Nine Eyes of Light* by Padam Aon Prakasha.

Tantric love: This concept is linked to the kundalini force. Sexual energy is the actual life force that is raised in energy through the union with the higher energies. It becomes a union of earthly and heavenly love and a way for the soul to mature. Often, tantra is described from the starting-point of earthly love between man and woman and how you as a couple, through uniting sexuality with a specific variation of meditation, are raised in soul together. When the kundalini force has been awoken, the union also happens from the other direction, which means that higher energies are anchored and grounded in the physical body.

Thymus: The thymus is a gland in the physical body above the breast cage. There is a connection between the endocrine system and the chakra system, and each chakra is linked to a specific gland. The thymus is located between the heart and throat chakras. To me as Barbro, the inner subtle flows made the thymus active when the energies from the heart were linked to Mikael´s and my different spiritual traditions and ways of speaking to the world. The energies from the heart and throat chakras merged and the thymus vibrated.

Universal love: There is personal love and universal love. These are connected and need to unite during our soul journey. We learn about love through our earthly relations. This experience enriches universal love. As earthly beings connected to universal love, we are able to love more in our personal relationships. The message of this book is that the development of the Earth and humanity needs to happen through ourselves – there are no shortcuts. Another example of this view (and also mentioned in the book) is Findhorn Foundation in the north of Scotland with its motto: 'Spirituality is love in practice.'

INSPIRATIONAL LITERATURE

Alexander, E (2012). *Proof of Heaven – A Neurosurgeon's Journey into the Afterlife*. London, UK: Piatkus.

Alexander, E (2014). *The Map of Heaven: How Science, Religion and Ordinary People Are Proving the Afterlife*. London, UK: Piatkus.

Alexander, E and Newell, K (2017). *Living in a Mindful Universe – A Neurosurgeon's Journey Into the Heart of Consciousness*. Rodale Books. USA: BooksMarketing@Rodale.com.

Botkin, A L (2005). *Induced After Life Communication*. Charlottesville, VA. USA: Hampton Roads Publishing.

Braden, G (2008). *The Divine Matrix: Bridging Time, Space, Miracles, and Believes*. Carlsbad, CA, USA: Hay House Inc.

Chopra, D (2006). *Life After Death: The burden of Proof*. London UK: Harmony/Penguin-Random House.

Crowley, J (2012). *Soul Body Fusion: The Missing Piece for Healing and Beyond*. Greenwood Village, CO, USA: Stone Tree Publishing.

Curman, M *(2012). Time please!* Sweden: LightSpira.

Curman, B *(2011). Head in Heaven*. Sweden: LightSpira.

Curman, B *(2018). Love Beyond Death*. Sweden: LightSpira.

Heartsong, C (2002). *Anna Grandmother of Jesus: A Message of Wisdom and Love*. London, UK: Hay House.

Kenyon, T & Sion, J (2002). *The Magdalen Manuscript: The Alchemies of Horus & the Sex Magic of Isis*. Orcas, WA, USA: ORB Communications.

Melchizedek, D (1999). *The Ancient Secret of The Flower of Life (Vol.1&2)*. Flagstaff, AZ, USA: Light Technology Publishing.

Melchizedek, D (2003). *Living in the Heart*. Flagstaff, AZ, USA. Light Technology Publishing.

Melchezidek, D (2007). *Serpent of Light: Beyond 2012 – The Movement of the Earth's Kundalini and the Rise of the Female Light, 1949 – 2013*. San Francisco, CA, USA. Red Wheel/Wieser.

Moody, A R (2001). *Life after Life*. New York City, NY, USA. Harper Collins.

Newton, M (2000). *Destiny of Souls: New Case Studies of Life Between Lives*. Woodbury, MN, USA: Llewellyn.

Newton, M (2009). *Memories of the Afterlife: Life Between Lives Stories of Personal Transformation.* Woodbury, MN, USA: Llewellyn.

Prakasha, P A (2010). *The Nine Eyes of Light: Ascension Keys from Egypt.* Berkley, CA, USA: North Atlantic Books.

Prakasha, P A & Prakasha, A A (2011). *Womb Wisdom.* Toronto, Canada: Destiny Books.

Tronick, E (2007). *The Neurobevhavioral and Social-Emotional Development of Infants and Children.* NYC, NY: W.W. Norton & Company.

ACKNOWLEDGEMENTS

Union of Souls is the second book in a trilogy about Mikael´s and my soul journeys. Several of you, whom I wish to thank, have been with me during the creation of both *Love Beyond Death* and *Union of Souls*. Within our soul fellowship, you have supported me in a variety of ways through your special talents and always with heart and care. Besides those of you that I mention here, friends have invested time in reading my manuscript and given me their feedback. I thank you for this valuable work! This unified force has carried me through the creation of the book.

Doris Ankarberg
Your sharp and clear clairvoyance have been an invaluable help for me throughout many years. Therefore, it was natural for me to turn to you a couple of months after Mikael´s death. You were there for me in understanding the feeling of being like a person cut in half after having lost the man of my life. You conveyed Mikael´s presence and words just as clearly from the other side. It was a relief and it made me trust what I myself was experiencing. Thank you!

Niklas Curman
You created the pictures that precede each chapter. You have a natural feel for how the pictures will amplify the message of the book. It is a pleasure to be able to work with you in putting the book together as a whole. You being family has made it even more joyful to work together. Thank you!

Kim Farnell
Being a native English speaker, you have worked with my manuscript to make the English language flow. You did the same with my book *Head in Heaven*. I am happy

that you are again on my team producing *Union of Souls.* Thank you!

Ulla Lindgren
You have been part of the team that translated my inner images to the cover of the book. As an artist and soul friend, you helped design the book to make the energy and message clear and understandable to other people. You work with great enthusiasm and joy. Thank you!

Marina Munk
Mikael and I met you in the early 1980s. There was a long gap when you were in the Amazon, although we visited you there for a few weeks in the middle of the 1990s. You returned to Scandinavia and then Sweden in 2009. Soon afterwards, we met again during a phase when I was in great need of help and guidance. For many years, I have regularly visited you for individual consultations and as part of different groups. You were also my travel guide for the journeys to Tibet, Peru and Bolivia and Egypt. All of this has been vital to be able to lift myself to those energies where Mikael and I can meet and develop together. Thank you!

Katarina Persson
We met in the summer of 2015 when I was going through what I called my 'trial of fire'. It was the start of a journey where Mikael´s and my soul relationship was given support that opened us even more to life´s mysteries. Your incredible breadth of working so naturally in the universal realm while at the same time keeping both your feet on the ground has allowed me to relax and appreciate the greatness of it all. Thank you!

The Seven Group
As my close colleagues, you followed and supported me in my day-to-day life through Mikael's death, funeral

and all that happened after. Few workplaces would have cared for me as you did. I could be myself with you in the roller-coaster of life. You have been like a warm embrace to me. Thank you!

Justo Viscarra

As a naturalist practitioner from the Aymara tribe, trained in traditional Bolivian medicine, you helped me as early as in 2008 to 'find my flower'. Much later, I understood that it had to do with the 'inner marriage', uniting the masculine and the feminine principles within me. You have the history and power of the Andes within you. You were close to Mikael and to me in our soul meetings by Lake Titicaca. Thank you!

Marie Örnesved

We have a long and valuable co-creation behind us through your company LightSpira. You helped Mikael to reach out with his message through his books and now you are producing my third book within LightSpira. How well you know us both. Now publishing *Union of Souls* both in Swedish and in English, you do the actual hands-on work. You also lead the creative team working with the book design. Your vision and concrete work of creating ways to spread heartful messages to the world is resonating with the content of the books, creating an invitation to a global meaningful co-creation far beyond each book in your network.

making messages from
loving hearts
available to a global audience

cocreators @lightspira.com
www.lightspira.com

www.ingramcontent.com/pod-product-compliance
Lightning Source LLC
Chambersburg PA
CBHW051306120626
46547CB00015B/2119